D0389114

WITHDRAWN

praise for the works of
d. watkins

"Our generation is seeking honest, courageous thought leaders and yearning for solutions to this country's seemingly hopeless race problem. D. Watkins is the former, and *The Beast Side* offers so much of the latter. It's a necessary read and the perfect bridge for the older and younger generations trying to make a change."—Issa Rae, actress, writer, producer, and creator of HBO's *Insecure*, on *The Beast Side*

"The thread that connects *The Cook Up* with the author's previous true-to-life treatise, *The Beast Side*...is, to me, of greater importance: It is Watkins's belief in the telling of Black stories, in their ugliness and in their beauty."
—Jason Parham, *New York Times*, on *The Cook Up*

"[D. Watkins] is not another elite voice for the voiceless. He is...an amplifier of low-income Black voices who have their own voices and have no problem using them. He dares us to listen." —Ibram X. Kendi, author of *How to Be an Anti-Racist*, on *We Speak for Ourselves*

"Watkins shows the Black community is not a monolith, even as we may wear the iconic T-shirts of the struggle yet have different thoughts about the issues faced. We are a diverse and proud community, trying to come to grips with who we are; sometimes wearing a mask within our own brother- and sisterhood." —April Ryan, author of *Under Fire*, on *We Speak for Ourselves*

"Watkins writes with a type of profound love for the Black forgotten that will compel all who read his timely words to never forget the Black people and places so many cultural critics and thought leaders disremember with ease."

—Darnell L. Moore, author of *No Ashes in the Fire*, on *We Speak for Ourselves*

"Amazing storytelling that brings us deep into the reality of East Baltimore…a moving and important piece of contemporary memoir." —Wes Moore, author of *The Work*, *The Other Wes Moore*, and *Five Days*, on *The Cook Up*

"That Watkins threaded his way from those corners to the page is rare enough. That he is so committed to pulling this world through with him—enough of it to at least rub our noses in it and make us acknowledge some collective responsibility— is precious." —David Simon, author of *The Corner* and creator of HBO's *The Wire*, on *The Cook Up*

"D. Watkins is uniquely equipped to communicate the political and social challenges of urban America, not only through the lens of academia but through empirical knowledge as well. He is the voice of the future seamlessly blending the wisdom of the streets and intellectual prowess in a way I have never experienced before."

—Jada Pinkett Smith, American actress, on *The Cook Up*

"An important story for both Black and white America, as well as this country's political leadership, to read if we're truly going to tackle the challenges that are facing our communities all across the country." —Chuck Todd, correspondent, NBC's *Meet the Press*, on *The Cook-Up*

Black Boy Smile

A Memoir in Moments

D. Watkins

LEGACY
LIT

New York Boston

Copyright © 2022 by D. Watkins

Cover design by Mikea Hugley. Cover photos © Devin Allen.

Cover copyright © 2022 by Hachette Book Group, Inc.

Hachette Book Group supports the right to free expression and the value of copyright. The purpose of copyright is to encourage writers and artists to produce the creative works that enrich our culture.

The scanning, uploading, and distribution of this book without permission is a theft of the author's intellectual property. If you would like permission to use material from the book (other than for review purposes), please contact permissions@hbgusa.com. Thank you for your support of the author's rights.

Legacy Lit, an imprint of Grand Central Publishing
Hachette Book Group
1290 Avenue of the Americas, New York, NY 10104
LegacyLitBooks.com
Twitter.com/LegacyLitBooks
Instagram.com/LegacyLitBooks

First edition: May 2022

Grand Central Publishing is a division of Hachette Book Group, Inc. The Legacy Lit and Grand Central Publishing names and logos are trademarks of Hachette Book Group, Inc.

The publisher is not responsible for websites (or their content) that are not owned by the publisher.

The Hachette Speakers Bureau provides a wide range of authors for speaking events. To find out more, go to www.hachettespeakersbureau.com or call (866) 376-6591.

Library of Congress Cataloging-in-Publication Data has been applied for.

ISBNs: 978-0-3069-2400-2 (hardcover) 978-0-3069-2399-9 (ebook)

Printed in the United States of America

LSC-C

Printing 1, 2022

For Dad,
you've been through more than most,
and strangely make all of this life stuff look
easy, too easy.
If I end up being half as great as you—
I'll be forever grateful.

contents

a note to the reader

Some names in this book have been changed to protect the innocent and guilty. Certain quotes and conversations have been reconstructed from memory.

a letter to my daughter

Dear Cross,

I love you.
    I've loved you since May 14, 2019, the day when your mother asked me to buy a pregnancy test. No one in the world knows their body better than your mother—she can feel a cold coming on three weeks before hacking out the first cough. So, when she asked for the test, disappeared into the bathroom, and reappeared with her smile, the smile that makes me fall in love over and over again, the smile you inherited—I knew you were coming, and that love grew. And that love will continue to grow and fill my spirit in ways I've never known, and I may never fully be able to understand its depths—but if I am ever to attempt, then I must go back to the beginning.
    This is the beginning of you.

introduction: the lie

"In patriarchal culture males are not allowed simply to be who they are and to glory in their unique identity."
—bell hooks, *The Will to Change*

"My muva and grandmuva make the best seafood salad for reallllll, I'm tellin' you," Kavon said. The streets nicknamed him Burger, because he was big, dark brown, and lumpy, with a flat spotty face that looked just like an overcooked burger. Burger was only a few years older, but triple my size. "Shit is *soooooooooooo* good, man, don't debate me," he spat, stuffing the mashed-up shrimp deep into his mouth, globs of wet mayonnaise oozing down his wide puffy jaws.

"Mmmmmmmmmm, mmmm, mmmmmmm," he groaned, wiping the chunky off-white filth away from the corners of his mouth.

It was about two weeks before our first day of school. We were posted on the corner of Ashland Avenue, in front of a slouched redbrick collapsing row house that had been boarded up longer than any of us could remember. All us boys were baked a shade darker than our real complexions from riding our bikes, hooping, and swimming at the rec center in the ninety-degree weather every day. The happy bunch of us were all summertime ashy in tank tops with socks pulled up to our knees. Burger eclipsed our edge of the block as he shoved more of that cocktail of canned shrimp, corner store mayo, and imitation crab-meat-shit that he swore was seafood salad into his nasty mouth. He was spooning it out of a tan faded plastic Country Crock bowl that used to be a margarine container a long time ago—everybody from our block used them as bowls when the fake butter inside had run out.

"That stuff stink!" I accidentally mumbled. *Shit.* Fear instantly shot through me as the thought escaped my mouth. *What in the fuck is wrong with me?* Every kid in the neighborhood knew Burger could beat the shit out of everybody, even the adults, and he was glad to, for any reason—we all held countless stories detailing the way Burger swung his puffy scarred mitts against somebody's teeth, so why would I comment, unless I wanted to be next? *Did I lose my fuckin' mind?*

My friend Troy who was with us looked at me like I had three heads with a "Are you fucking crazy?" face and then went back to his Game Boy. As my heart sank into the bottom of my stomach, all I could hear was Troy's bony fingers clicking away on Mario Brothers, and Burger shoving more of that shit into his mouth like, "Muuuuuuuummmmmmmm, so good."

Burger was a bully in every sense of the word. He always started fights and finished them. He was bigger than grade school teachers, bigger than the principal, and bigger than his big brother, who was also a bully. We were only friends with him to avoid being on the wrong side of his fist. Once he'd run up on the school bus and knocked out the driver. POW! Burger's fist blasted right on top of his face. The driver went straight to sleep and only the ambulance crew and their fists full of ammonia tablets could wake him. He'd only done that because someone had dared him to. That was Burger, and that's the kind of things Burger liked to do. Pissing him off had me so shook that I could've shit myself, until I realized that he probably didn't hear me.

After Burger sopped up the last of the "seafood" salad, he trained his eyes on Troy's Game Boy. "I wanna play, yo, I got next," he said, snatching it out of Troy's hands. Troy and I were the only kids in the neighborhood with Game Boys, as most parents didn't have $90 to spend on a handheld game console. But what Burger's mom couldn't buy him, he took.

"Come on, man! I was about to win Mario!" Troy protested.

Burger shrugged, looked at Troy, and breathed, "I should sell this shit."

"Come on, man!" Troy pleaded.

Us kids were just starting to see the effects of crack cocaine, or what the streets called ready rock, ready, or crack—a cheaper, rock-like, smokable form of powder cocaine. Crack hit our neighborhood like a missile, and nobody saw it coming. Respected coaches, the flyest uncles, and the prettiest teenage girls had morphed into funky, stealing, toothless addicts that roamed the block like zombies all day and night looking for crack. Many of the top dealers were teenagers driving brand-new Acura Legends, Nissan Pathfinders, 300Zs, and 5 Series BMWs, bossing other kids, beating the snot and shit out of grown men begging for a rock, and fucking bent-over grown women in the alley who needed a blast. Kids like me, Troy, and Burger were the young soldiers, next in line—so we had to be tough, because the older kids were always watching, offering us money, work, making sure we represented the neighborhood and carried ourselves like men.

We weren't men, and didn't really want to be men, we

wanted to be kids, but had to always act like men, whatever that meant—it was all a lie. And I quickly learned how to be a liar. As a matter of fact, I mastered it.

"Yo, give it back!" Troy yelled at Burger, who was holding his Game Boy up in the air out of our reach. "Come on, I was about to win! Give it back, yo!"

Burger laughed, mushed Troy's forehead against the brick wall, and put the game into his pocket. Defeated, Troy slumped down on the steps and wrapped his face up inside of both of his hands. A few girls, Nay Nay, Mia, Ki Ki, and Lil Shannon, made their way over to the corner. Burger, realizing that he had a more attractive audience now, whipped the Game Boy back out.

"Y'all freaks wanna free Game Boy?" he teased. Collectively, they all rolled their eyes and popped their necks in annoyance.

I looked in Troy's eyes, saw them filling, becoming wet glossy slits, hungry to spill over—Burger had tested us before, knocked us down, gave us wedgies and wet willies, but he never took anything from us, he took things from other kids all of the time, but not us, because we were a part of his crew. This was new, and painful.

"Let me give your lil game back," Burger said, approaching Troy on the steps. "You look like you gonna cry, like a lil bitch. Why you always around him, D? He a bitch!"

"He ain't a bitch," I pushed back, regretfully.

Troy looked away. The girls were scribbling hopscotch squares in the middle of the street with broken-off pieces of fat chalk when they stopped to look. Nay Nay's expression toward me mirrored a deer's gaze in the brightest of headlights. I liked her, so though I was scared, my fear masqueraded as rage. I swallowed my throat, feeling the sweat form into dots of Braille that stretched across my forehead. "Burger, why you gotta be so extra all of the time, man?" I said with my chest poked out and my face twisted into an angry question mark. "Give his fuckin' game back!"

That was the start of my lie, knowingly pretending that I wasn't terrified.

Instead of pummeling me on the spot, Burger turned and spit a piece of shrimp shell that must have been resting in between his jumbled teeth onto Troy's face. The warm slimy shell that was the size of a flake stuck to the center of his forehead and everyone watched as it slid down his nose, leaving a slippery trail.

"Ewwwwwwww," one of the girls shouted. "He nastyyyyyy!"

Burger erupted in triumphant laughter.

Troy wiped his face, and caught the tear that finally slipped out.

"Yo, leave him alone, Burger—you fat bitch, what the fuck!" I yelled.

"Chill, yo!" Troy shouted.

And suddenly I felt my body being swooped into the heavens and then planted deeply into the roots of the concrete, followed by a hailstorm of fists tagging my nose, forehead, and both of my eyes. As he beat me, Burger dug into my pockets. This was his reward system, what he had earned for stomping me out—he got me for a few dollars, my Now and Laters, Lemonheads, and everything else I had. I managed to break away, running down Ashland Avenue faster than Flo Jo.

. Burger was yelling after me, "You bitch-ass nigga! You can't come around here no more!"

I kept running and running and running, feeling my eye tighten as tears dried down my cheeks.

I ran up all the way through Madeira Street, down Jefferson, over to Robinson where I lived. "D, what's wrong, are you okay?" a couple of people asked during my marathon. I only stopped briefly to say, "I'm great!"—they knew that I was lying. Anyone with eyes could clearly see that I wasn't okay by the look of despair tattooed on my face, a look I've never learned to hide. My broken facial expression created the foundation that my lies were built on as I grew from a boy to a man. It became my default.

I don't have a poker face; my egghead and my blank stare that drifts off into space mirror exactly how I feel on the inside. When I'm angry, my forehead slopes and the meat under my eyebrows puffs up—this is when I shut down. I don't talk. I struggle to think past anything that isn't revenge. And when I'm happy, my cheeks inflate like party balloons and sit on top of a smile wide enough to wrap around my entire head— this is when I open up. I can't stop talking. I struggle to think past anything that doesn't involve me emptying my wallet and giving everything to everyone around me. My pain, like my joy, has always been clearly visible, yet I lie. The lies are self-justified by understanding that the *Are-you-okay?* askers can't do anything anyway. The Burgers of the world could and would steal your money and beat the shit out of you, too.

When I got home, I headed straight toward the bathroom to clean myself up. Once inside, I locked the door and then stared at myself in the mirror—on the other side was everything a man wasn't, a chump with a bruised face and a knot the size of a tennis ball forming above my eyelid.

"What happened to your eye?" Mom asked, as soon as I exited the bathroom.

"Dammmmmmmmn," Dad enthusiastically followed, sipping a Coke. "Dammmmmmmmn!"

"I fell down playing basketball," I lied, on my way into hiding.

———

I was a prisoner in my home for over a week after the attack. I ran like a punk, was humiliated, and felt like I didn't deserve to go outside or have fun with the rest of the kids, doing the things that kids in the summer do. I could see Burger's blubbery jaws bouncing up and down, laughing at me. I could hear Nay Nay along with the girls clutching their stomachs as they laughed too at the way I ran, without fighting back. I wanted to stay locked away in my room forever, but school was starting in a few days and I knew I would eventually have to confront them all.

"Are you ready for school?" my mother asked. "This summer blew by."

"It did," I answered.

"What's wrong?" she asked. "I know when something is wrong with you."

"I'm fine," I said.

"Okay, you figured that lock out yet?"

I pulled the Master Lock out, held it up in front of her—three times one way, two times the other way, and straight to the last number, *click*. She raised her thin eyebrows in that *I'm impressed* gesture and made her way down the hall. I laid back on my bed and watched my dusty ceiling fan whip around and around. I wasn't being who I was supposed to be. *I don't get bullied*, I thought, *I shouldn't fear anyone, I am me*.

And then it all came to me one night while binge watching a day's worth of cartoons and sitcoms that destiny was mine,

I was responsible for my own hero story. From *Transformers* to *The Fresh Prince of Bel-Air* to *Boyz n the Hood*, the hero always had victory, as long as he had a plan. I needed to do something that no one else was willing to do to erase the icky feeling that Burger left me with. I needed to win.

So I took the lock that my mom had given me, dropped it into a long sock, and tied it into a knot. Then I put on my Nike Air Max sneakers, which were much lighter than all of my Jordans and the shoes that I could run the fastest in—and I bolted over to Madeira, swinging the long knotted sock like nunchakus. Burger, along with some of the girls, including Nay Nay, a bunch of other kids, a collection of addicts, and the dealers that always decorated the block were there. Everything was the same, nothing had changed in my absence. Burger was knee-deep in a dice game with some older dudes, sweating like a hog, screaming his point, rattling dice and picking loose bills up off of the ground. I was surprised to see Troy clicking away at his Game Boy. I didn't know he'd be coming to the corner without me.

"'Sup, Troy?" I asked.

"What you 'bout to do, D?" Troy grimaced, safely securing his Game Boy in his pocket.

Burger looked up from his game, and our eyes met. He laughed and turned back to toss the dice against the wall. I winded up the sock, aimed, and cracked a healthy chunk of meat out of the back of his head. POW! He slapped the pavement like a sack of trash. After the first blow, I hit him again, this time harder, hard enough to redden us with his blood as I whipped again and again, basking in the carnage. I didn't hear anything—a silence blanketed my surroundings. I blacked out, cracking him again and again and again—then a clapping crowd shook me out of my trance, and I heard kids singing my praises, cheering at the slain menace. A few older dudes rushed to yank me away and scooped up Burger so that he didn't bleed out. Word on the streets was that he got 180 staples and stitches after my blows.

Victory! Victory! Victory—a lie.

Burger whipped my ass at least twenty or more times after that. And to make matters worse, hitting Burger didn't protect Troy or make me feel any better. It did make me look better in front of my peers and homies; Nay Nay even kissed me on the lips a week later. But I felt like a terrible person. And knowing this, I continued to choose violence—like a wave of destruction that I continued to ride for most of my life. But this is what it took to handle all things like "a man," like the men in my family, and on TV—you had to pretend that fear and regret didn't exist.

Years later, while passing a blunt around on a corner with some friends, close to where the beatdown took place, someone said that Burger had been gunned down for hustling on another dude's block. I snickered and said something like, "That fat-ass nigga always had his hands on something that wasn't his." Everyone on the corner laughed while agreeing. We'd grown up with Burger, he was one of us. He was an asshole, but he was ours. We spent years with him playing basketball, talking to girls, and just being kids—but the lie did not allow us to acknowledge our loss. We were hurt, saddened by his death, but we could not show it; that wasn't allowed, we had to take it like men. We said "Fuck 'em" and went on with our conversation, our lives—feeding, clothing, providing, nourishing the lie as men.

This lie has been told for generations—strangling the emotions of Black men everywhere, forcing us to hold back our tears, our smiles, our joy, and reject feeling anything, at least too much or much at all. I bought into this act for too long, and now, after decades of it, before and after the death of Burger, I'm finally at a place where I want to abandon the lie. I want to bury it. I want to freely experience joy and love and hurt, to stop using trauma like a currency.

What I learned from cracking Burger in the head with a Master Lock, or from the years of crack sales and the rest of the madness that came next, is that it was all a lie. None of it made me happy. I was taught to use the violence that accompanies toxic masculinity as my own personal painkiller, as if aggression could heal, and I was tired. I don't want to be a liar. I don't want to be the hero.

What I want?

I want to smile.

BOOK I

a camp story

9 years old, 1989

Someone stole my innocence, but I'm a
Black boy, so no one cared.

1

"Lil nigga, you probably ain't had pussy since it had you!" my camp counselor Heavy breathed into my ear, squeezing my nine-year-old shoulders and pushing me through the cabin door, into a dim-lit room. "Don't come out until she tell you to come out!"

I slowly stepped forward into the room. A song I heard too many times—at block parties and cookouts—whispered out of a small black-and-gray plastic radio with a wire-hanger antenna sitting on the dresser.

Back to life, back to reality,
back to the here and now...

"Boy, stop lookin' all stupid and close the door," a raspy voice shouted over the music. "Lock it."

I followed her directions without facing her, holding the thin door, wiggling it shut, latching it. And then I stood there, paralyzed, waiting for another order. She brushed past me on her way to the bed, bumping my shoulder. Finally, I saw her. She was a woman, but about my height. Her thighs thicker than my torso. Her odor, like stale minty-musty sweat, filled the room.

"Won't you sit down?" she asked, looking at me. I looked away. "What cabin you in?"

She was brown, almond. Again I noticed that she was a woman, not a girl; double my size and my age, I thought. Her big white teeth poked out when she spoke, half of them separated by gaps so large that I could probably have fit my thumb in between. She was wearing a loud neon pink tennis skirt that floated above her upper thighs. She sat with her legs open wide in front of me.

"Thirteen–fifteen," I responded.

The older guys, the ones who hung at the top of my block—they loved women. They laughed with them, drove them places, showed off the things they'd bought for them. They fought with them, and told the women that they loved them. I didn't love this lady. I didn't want to do anything for this lady. She was a stranger.

"Oh okay, well, how old is you, boy? You look like a little baby," she said, with one eyebrow raised.

"I'm nine and a half," I replied, looking away.

She laughed so hard a mist of spit sprayed from her mouth. Holding her stomach, she laughed some more, each chuckle carrying her head up and down in a rupture, with her long cleavage jiggling in waves with each movement.

"Yeah, okay, boy. I know ya big-ass self older than that. Come over here, boy," she ordered.

My heart sank to my feet. Beads of sweat stretched across my forehead and drizzled down the side of my face. My shoes felt like fifty-, no, seventy-five-pound weights, and I trudged toward her.

"Nine and a half years old," she laughed. "Boy, you silly."

I stood about a foot away from her as she started to pull me toward her. I felt myself being sucked deeper into her world. A world of sweat and stickiness. She smelled like Ashland Avenue. Or like what Grandma meant when she'd put her face close to mine, and say, "You smell like outside, go wash up."

She stuck her hands up the bottom of my basketball shorts. And rubbed me.

I looked away. I wanted her to stop. Or did I? I felt as bad as the room smelled, as bad as she smelled, like chewing gum and eggs. Crickets screamed through the window as blood rushed into my fingers, my toes, the tip of my penis. My body clearly did not want her to stop.

The older dudes from the top of my block...I thought of them. They'd pin her to the bed, flesh thirsty, fearless. They'd rip her panties off with their teeth and dive in. They talked about it all the time on the block. I was their lil homie, I was supposed to be like them.

So why am I scared?

Why isn't she scared?

The older dudes from the top of my block...They'd always joke that one day it would be my turn to fuck, to taste it, to "Dip my head in the devil's ass," they'd say. I never imagined it like this...with a girl I didn't know...who was older...a girl who was not my girlfriend...a girl I never had a crush on...a girl I never wrote notes to or drew pictures for...a girl who smelled like outside.

She rubbed me. And for the first time, I was being touched; it was strange for a Black boy like me where hugs, kisses, and "I love you"s at home were rarely traded, if ever at all. Now the only things separating me from this stranger touching me were my fear and the smells of Isoplus Oil Sheen, Speed Stick, Big Red chewing gum, and Pink Oil Moisturizer.

"Don't think you fuckin' me," she laughed. "I gotta man back home from up Park Heights, *da-hahaha.*" One warm clammy hand was on me, squeezing me; her other hand was searching for the radio dial, turning up the music.

However do you want me,
However do you need me.

"You got long eyelashes, just like a little girl," she laughed, squinting her eyes and focusing on my face. "Heavy told you how this work, right?" she asked, smiling. I caught a glimpse of her round face again. Her forehead was way too small for her eyebrows, they almost touched.

"Some of my lil girls look out for him, and some of his lil boys look out for me, *da-haha.* You scared, ain't chu?"

I imagined her boyfriend, a twenty-something-year-old with a mustache and a real chest, not a frail chest like mine, but a fully developed one, like those on the action figures my mom bought me, that I never played with. Her man probably had a car, a Benz, or a 300Z with a T-Top, or a Nissan Path-finder, or a 4Runner. If she had a "man," what did she want with a boy like me?

"Sit on the bed," she ordered, pulling me by my dick until it hurt, until I was closer to her.

She flipped her skirt up and caressed herself, pulling her panties to the side, looking at the ceiling. I looked, even though I felt like I shouldn't. I had never seen a vagina before—well, a real one. I saw them in magazines that my older cousins had. They would fuck every woman in between those pages, they'd declare. But they'd never meet those women, and if they did, they wouldn't even know what to say to say them.

I couldn't really see hers, the room was dark, but I could smell it. Her crotch was dark and hairy. There were fingers, and smacking sounds, and stink, and moans.

I stood still as the moment blurred.

What if someone walked in? I wished someone would.

2

Carefully. Slowly.

I angled my foot out of the new Jordans—my *new* Jordans.
I did it the same every night—slowly eased out of my sneakers, and then I examined them. Starting with the right shoe,
holding it close to my chest like a newborn, I eyed the stitch-
ing, the seams, and used my index finger to scratch away any
crud or dirt that clung to them. I had to protect the suede.
I dabbed a soapy rag across and around any imperfections or
evidence of my day. A sauce splatter wiped off easy; oil scuffs,
not so much. If my midsoles were dirty, which was rare for
me, I took the special toothbrush that I only used for my
sneakers and scrubbed, scrubbed, scrubbed all of the visible
blemishes away. Then I placed them on top of the box they
came in—boxes I never trashed—to dry.

Air Jordans were the first thing in my life I ever remember
obsessing over. Before I knew anything about Michael Jordan,
this kid named Ant who lived three doors over hit the block
with a pair of white 3s on. As he walked, my eyes followed
his feet from the corner, to his house, and back to the corner,
where I ran up on him to get a closer look. "Yo, what kina
shoes is those?" He said the shoes were specially made for the
best player to ever touch a basketball—ever. The leather was

tumbled and then smoothed and sealed with elephant skin. The most beautiful shoes I ever saw in my eight years of life. I was lovesick, and spent sleepless nights contemplating about how to get them. My dad bought me my first pair the day after I saw Ant's.

My mother came into my room while I was restuffing the new Jordans with the white crinkly tissue paper that comes inside of all Nike sneakers, the paper that maintains the form. We don't do bent sneakers on my block. "Hey," Ma said, wearing her it's-Friday-and-the-direct-deposit-just-hit smile. A smile that was clearly too big for her button face. It wasn't Friday, so the smile made me worry.

"I found a really cheap camp out in the woods to send you to this summer!" she said, swinging her arms. Standing next to my stack of Nike boxes that were twice her height, looking like a schoolgirl my age.

"I don't wanna go."

"All of your cousins will be there! You guys will have so much fun, there are basketball courts, a beach, *everything*," she exclaimed. "Your cousins will be there, you *are* going."

I loved my cousins—Lo Lo, Lil Chuckie, and especially Kevin—but I didn't really care if they were going to be there or not. I didn't want to go to a camp, or pretend that I was happy to go with them. I never thought about spending time in the woods, or even wanted to. People on TV went to camp in the woods, but that was TV, not real life.

In real life summer is block ball, crate ball, Truth or Dare, and 7-11, which means the girl you like gives you seven kisses and eleven dry humps; Big Eric's block party, frozen cups and brain freezes, Hutch and Mongoose trick bikes, and neon Nikes.

"Just keep ya money, Ma, I'm good."

She told me I was going anyway. And left the room.

I reexamined my Jordans, placed them gently back in their box.

––––––––

School ended a week later, and I was sitting shotgun in the car with Dad, aka Big Dwight, with my seat a little leaned back as usual. My shoes propped up on top of my black Nike duffel bag loaded with camp clothes, shorts and tank tops, listening to his slow jams—Al Green, Luther, Frankie Beverly, and the rest of the songs that only bumped on 95.9, the radio station for old Black people. He liked to tilt the roof up, just enough for the sun to gleam over his waves. He obsessed over his curls for hours every day with all types of grease, sheen, and exotic oils, usually sealed tight under his do-rag, all the way up till he did the big reveal, peeling the cap off, making us seasick with the dark waves he had worked so hard on.

"Do you really wanna go?" he asked.

I didn't want to go, but I didn't want to look scared either.

But I was scared.

I was raised in an environment where fear was lied about, even if you were nine years old. I'd never been away from my family, or even outside of Baltimore, so any other place my fear could have been natural. But it wasn't for me. The people I respected taught me that fear was the worst thing a man could feel. I had to hold it during the drive, and it felt like I was the only person in the world capable of harvesting this weak emotion, so I did what any guy in this situation would do: I lied.

"I'm not scared of anything," I said, with a straight face.

"Good, you shouldn't be," he said. "But I didn't ask you if you were scared, I asked if you really wanted to go."

I looked at my feet. Last year's Jordans—the fire-red version of the 3s. The same as Ant had last year, and just as clean and new. Classics now. My new-new Jordans were in my bag. My 3s had a bit of a crinkle in the center now because I wore them so much. I'd laced them with the whitest shoestrings anybody has ever seen. I washed them in Clorox, then let them soak in a cup of Clorox overnight, before washing them in Clorox again. "It seems like we never have any bleach," my mom commented one day, scratching her head.

"I don't wanna go, Dad, I don't care about a fucking camp," I said. "I told Ma it sounds stupid, like, why I gotta do this? Why me?"

"Well, I think you should try new things. I've never been to camp," he said. "Maybe you'll like it."

Fathers have one job. It looks like many jobs—but all of the jobs fall under the same umbrella: Protect.

Fathers are supposed to protect.

I slung my duffel over my left shoulder and we walked toward the pickup location at this west Baltimore church. A bunch of kids were standing in front in a collage of brown— boys, girls, fat kids with acne, skinny kids, long-faced kids, young and older kids, some bald, others hairy. They wore bright-colored Nike, Fila, and Etonics and carried big luggage, or stuffed book bags that wouldn't zip shut, and duffels like mine, or trash bags—so many kids had their belongings in trash bags.

I scanned the crowd, not a cousin in sight.

"Didn't Ma say some of my cousins were comin' too?"

"She definitely told me that," Dad replied. "You'll be okay, though." He spread his arms wide and wrapped them around me—squeezing me breathless, burying my fade into his chest. He said to call him if anything went wrong. I played it cool as I bopped off, my bag in hand. I glanced back; he stood by his car swinging his hand in a slow wave. I shot him a peace sign and got on the bus.

We were both scared, we couldn't say how scared we were.

———

After the longest bus ride of my life with a bunch of kids I didn't know, a wooden sign that read "Camp Farthest Out" greeted us as we pulled into a parking lot next to another group of buses. The kids bolted off. One hour had felt like ten hours. I didn't know *what* I was pulling into.

Camp Farthest Out was established in 1962 with the purpose of "providing a camping experience for a wide range of disadvantaged youths of all races and creeds," according to its mission statement. The thirty-seven-acre camp site was situated in the Carroll County section of Sykesville, Maryland, and allegedly provided "healthful surroundings in the great outdoors, with a nature trail, an in-ground swimming pool, a playing field, and a basketball court," just like my mom said.

"Line up!" a neckless, wide, tree-stump-shaped man yelled. "Shut up and line up!" he said again to us kids. "The quicker we get you into your cabins, the quicker we can start our two weeks of fun!"

A group of mid-teens and early twenty-somethings in khaki shorts and tattered sneakers assembled in front of us. I scanned the crowd—again, no cousins. Just a sea of brown faces, even more now with all the buses unloaded, all strangers.

People looked at me. I looked at them. Some with direct eye

contact and others eyeing my sneakers. A few pointed them out to the person that they were talking to.

It felt like everybody had somebody, except me.

"Nigga! What the fuck yew lookin' at!" a short, pretty-eyed girl in pink spat in my direction. "I'll get yew fucked up!"

"Huh?" I replied.

"Ya lil freak-ass, lil dick-suckin' whore! Shit-ball lil bitch, fuck you!" screamed a lanky, long-toothed guy over my shoulder.

She charged past me with an overhand right, and the guy bobbed, grabbed her arm, and sent her spiraling until she tripped and slid into the dirt. Her pink was now dust brown. She popped back up, rushing again, only to be intercepted by a female counselor. A male counselor grabbed the long-toothed dude by his neck and squeezed until we could see every long tooth inside of the kid's mouth; he must have had sixty molars. His busted track shoes dangled as the man-sized counselor lifted him off of the ground.

"Don't get killed before the week out!" the counselor yelled.

I put my head down. I'd have to get through these two weeks without being choked out, or "killed."

"Oh, he was here last summer, that dude don't play," some boy behind me mumbled.

The cabins were based on gender and age. Each of the counselors held up cards—the seven- to ten-year-old boys were to go with the man holding the 7–10 card, and seven- to ten-year-old girls were to bunk with the lady, but I decided to line up with the thirteen- to fifteen-year-olds. My cousins were a few years older than me, so if they did make it to the camp, I would be in their group.

I towered over most nine-, ten-, and eleven-year-olds, with a size 10 shoe, so no one questioned my age. Unfortunately, the counselor for thirteen- to fifteen-year-olds was the neckless stump guy. His name was Heavy.

"Get in a straight line and follow me to the cabin!" Heavy instructed. "Get out of line, get fucked up!"

We marched to one of the many cabins on the boys' side of the site. The inside was lined with wall-to-wall beds, the thin kind like those in jails or military bases on television. The other boys wasted no time claiming bunks. I flopped my bag on a vacant bed near the center.

"Yo, my cousin bed is next to yours, let me get that so I can be by my cousin," said a tall pie-faced boy. He had man-sized shoulders and a thousand freckles. He was built like an uncle, stockier than everybody in the cabin. I thought the kid was too yellow to be Black, like he was mixed with something, but he had to be Black, because everybody else was. I didn't push back, I just picked up my bag and found another bed across the room. Him and his cousin burst out laughing.

As we settled, I noticed again that everybody seemed to be laughing and joking like they knew each other for years. I realized this camp was something they did every summer.

"Yo, Heavy, where da bathroom?" one of the kids asked.

"It's out the back door, and three minutes up that pathway," Heavy replied, pointing, jaws wobbling just like the meat that hung from his arms. "But at night, it's a bucket out back for you to piss in."

"Yuck!" a number of us said in unison.

"Aye! Aye! You can't go through dem woods at night!" Heavy screamed over us. "You can't go through dem woods at night!" he repeated. "The KKK is known to snatch up young niggas in doze woods!"

"What's a KKK?" a small mousy kid whispered to me.

"That's racist white people who dress up in all white sheets like ghosts and try to kill you," I replied. "I never seen any 'round my way. I really never see white people at all, except the cops."

"Shorty, shut the fuck up when I'm talkin'!" Heavy breathed in my direction, barreling through the crowd. "You think you tough?"

I stood silent.

"Fuck is you deaf?" he continued, stepping closer, eyeballs blood-beat red like he plucked them out of his head and soaked them in cheap vodka every night. His neck and shoulders straight, chest inflated, forehead and eyebrows clenched into an angry fist.

With one swing he knocked away the two boys in front of me to get closer, foam and spit-ash growing around his mouth.

"Nah, I ain't deaf," I said. "You told us to shut the fuck up."

The cabin shook with boys' laughter, and "Yo crazzzzzies!"

Next thing I knew Heavy's arms were wrapped around my neck. I was in a headlock, my forehead lost in his arm meat, my breath slipping away, the cabin still laughing, harder now. "You still funny, nigga?" he asked, squeezing my head tighter, his slimy arm fluid oozing into my face, my hair, my nostrils, my mouth. Smothered, I was fading. He dumped me on the floor.

The fire in me wanted to pop up, square up with my chin dipped, and give him an overhand right, a left, and another right to knock him on his fat ass.

I wanted that respect, that fear—I wanted the other people in the cabin to fear me, like I feared them.

But I just laid there, balled up, defeated.

"Where you from, lil nigga?" Heavy breathed, standing over me. "Never seen you, where you from?"

"Down the hill, nigga!" I barked, wiping his sweat off of me. "Down the hill."

"Ohhhhhhhhhhh!" they all yelled. "Yoooooo!" Heavy included.

"Yous a lil ova east nigga!" Heavy laughed. "Boy, this a Murphy Fuckin' Homes cabin!"

Murphy Homes was a housing project in west Baltimore, located near the church where the bus picked us up. All of these kids were strangers to me because they were from west Baltimore. East and west Baltimore are two different worlds. They might as well be two different planets—we don't come on their side, and they don't come on ours. There's no history on why we're so divided; however, I'd bet my money on it having something to do with Baltimore's historically poor public transportation. A ride from my east Baltimore block to the center of west Baltimore takes about thirteen minutes by car, and probably one and a half hours by bus.

"Okay, lil niggas!" Heavy yelled, dragging a small dingy towel across his face. "Line up, we gonna march down to meet with the rest of the campers for orientation."

"Get ya shit together, lil East Side," Heavy huffed in my direction. "This gonna be a long two weeks for you!"

———

We spiraled down a dusty trail of rocks and trampled grass—dirt brushed my Jordans. I wished for my cousins to appear; they would crack Heavy in the head with a baseball bat, they'd be happy to do it. They cared about me, and that's how they showed it. If my cousins were there, I thought, he wouldn't have ever put his hands on me.

But they weren't there, and they weren't coming, and I knew it.

I was alone and would have to figure it out alone.

"Yo, are you okay?" that mousy kid squeaked. "Hey man, what is your name?" he continued as if I hadn't ignored him, tapping my shoulder. "What they call you?"

"D," I said, without turning around. "And I'm good, fuck Heavy."

"I'm Antwan, everybody call me Twan. Heavy is okay for the most part, just don't give him a reason to mess with you."

Twan was bony, even skinner than I was, so skinny he didn't have shoulders. He had a flat fade, accompanied by a bird-ish face and mannerisms to match. He was from Murphy Homes housing project too, like every other kid in our bunk except me. He was also my age but opted to stay in his older cousin's group. His cousin was Jabari, the freckled pie-face guy that asked me to switch beds. I guess everybody was Jabari's cousin.

We reached the end of the trail where all the different age groups sat on the ground or on benches or chairs in front of an older Black man with salt-and-pepper hair, in one of those short-sleeved button-ups that only older Black men wear, with jeans and church shoes. He shared the laws of the land. No sex, no fighting, no drugs, no kissing, no touching, and the counselors, our "big brothers and sisters," were our judge and jury—and if we were bad, we weren't being sent home, so we shouldn't even think about acting up or out.

He continued with the shower rules, and how we'd learn to swim, become Red Cross certified, praise Jesus; and how we'd go on a five-mile hike, be fed three meals a day with dessert, hear camp stories, and play ball, and how we'd remember our time at Camp Farthest Out forever.

His speech was followed by a huge feast—crispy chicken nuggets with white meat inside, not the gray stuff I was used to, curly fries, chocolate cake, milk, juice, Neapolitan ice cream, and we could take as many servings as we wanted.

After dinner, we all challenged each other to foot races, and shared stories about our families, the sneakers we loved, and dirt bikes. I shared how I rode a PW50 and was going to get a CR80 when I got bigger. We revealed our crushes and what they looked like, being happy to be able to swim all day whenever we wanted, how good those nuggets were, and how good it felt to be out of our neighborhoods even though Heavy was probably going to knock all of our teeth out by the last day. I didn't want to come, but camp was starting to seem okay. I felt the power of independence—it was freeing in a way.

I returned to the cabin and stretched across my bunk, dozing off to a sound I had never heard in real life: crickets. It sounded like there were millions of crickets screaming through my window. In my neighborhood, sounds of nature were sirens and gunshots. Crickets were probably eaten by all of the mouse-sized cockroaches that were scattered all over the place.

Something crawled in my nose—it's a dream, back to sleep—no something definitely is in my nose. I swatted my face with my right hand, and heard boys giggling by my bedside. I felt something wet in my left hand and opened my eyes. My hand was covered in mustard.

"Yoooooo, I thought you was left-handed from how you hooped," a beady-eyed boy named Kareem chuckled, holding a perfectly twisted piece of paper. "You was supposed to smash mustard in ya face!"

Jabari was next to him, and passed me the squeezable

French's mustard bottle. "Come on, East Side, get the fuck up. You gotta help us get somebody now," he ordered, yanking me out of bed.

I wiped the mustard on a towel that belonged to the kid in the next bunk, and followed them across the room. The glow from the moon shone just enough for me to see through the rows of sleeping Black boy faces. We were all exhausted after dinner, likely from the bus ride, the racing, the chicken nuggets, the unspoken anxiety.

"Get him," Kareem whispered, pointing to a plump kid. "Look, get him."

The kid was in a deep sleep, resting flat on his back with his mouth wide open. The plan was to put some mustard in his hand while someone else used the twisted paper to tickle his nose, so that he'd react, rubbing mustard on his face. I thought it was stupid.

Kareem and Jabari made their way to their beds and got into position to pretend to be asleep as I screwed the top off of the mustard, centered the container above the plump kid's head, and dumped a glob of mustard right onto the center of his face. I don't know if he was dreaming or allergic to mustard or just scared, but he let out a scream like I'd never heard before, "TAAAAAAAAAAA! YAAAAAAAAAAA!" It sounded like a bag of baby kittens had been dropped into a pot of boiling grease. I jetted to my bed and dived under the paper-thin covers as everyone woke up wondering what the heck that was. Jabari even fake-rubbed his eyes like, "What's goin' on, yo? Why y'all so loud?"

As the fat kid started to wipe the mustard off with a shirt, our cabin rumbled with laughter.

We cackled loud until Heavy entered.

He made his way to the kid's bed, knocked the shirt out

of his hand, and punched him hard, knocking the mustard off of his face—knocking some blood out too. "Faggot," he yelled. "You fuckin' faggot!"

The laughing stopped, all of the noise stopped—we just sat there and watched Heavy pound until he was tired of pounding. "Keep cryin', bitch, and I'ma do it again!"

Finally, Heavy hunched his way back to his room, exhausted.

Kareem tucked his head under his cover and kept it there.

Jabari giggled.

I just watched.

3

The next morning the plump kid's bed was vacant and his bags were gone.

Rumors circulated about him being sent home or transferred to another cabin. It was all my fault. I was just messing around. I wasn't a bully. I hated bullies. I didn't want to pick on anyone. I never knew it would lead to a beating. *Heavy just plows through people as if there's no consequences*, I thought, *as if we don't have family that he'll have to answer to.*

"I got that lil bitch sent to another cabin," Heavy said to us as we lined up for breakfast, his big face still Brailled with beads of sweat, always wiping himself with a beige napkin or towel that used to be white. "Any other of you lil bitches wanna switch cabins?"

I wanted to raise my hand, I wanted to bunk with kids my age. By now I knew that my cousins weren't coming. *Nobody's coming, and these dudes are crazy*, I thought. Camp is bullshit, ain't no Jesus here. I told Ma, but she didn't listen, she never listens—maybe she'll listen if Heavy smashes my skull in and they send me home in a pine box.

Damn, I wanted to raise my hand. I couldn't, it was stuck. Fear had more power over it than me.

I knew my friends back home were sharing pizza, debating

Nikes, hooping and playing Catch-One-Catch-All and throw-up tackle and probably forgetting about me.

I asked one of the counselors if I could call home, and the answer was no.

———

The smell of the food took my mind off of Heavy's abuse, as we lined up in front of the cafeteria. Pork bacon, pork sausage, and perfectly round and stacked-up pancakes and French toast sticks were lined up in front of me at the center of a long wooden picnic-style table. I didn't even like pork. I was so hungry I know other people could hear my stomach growling for food. My mouth was drier than eczema—lips white and peeling like dried glue—and I was feeling lightheaded.

Enter Heavy's pudgy hands, fingering the assortment of brown sausages, snatching piles of food up like a monster, inhaling slabs of bacon, smashing broken pieces of pancake into the corners of his mouth.

He had to have about fifty thousand calories worth of food on his plate, enough for a small village. When he was done, the big kids bum-rushed the platters and swung elbows at us little dudes, grabbing our small faces and mushing us out of place.

I wanted pancakes, extra pancakes, and eggs and French toast, everything—but by the time I could finally get to the platters, Kareem and other big kids were on their second or third servings, spooning up the last of the eggs. Everything else was basically gone. It was just Twan and me standing there with empty plates.

"They got some cereal ova there for y'all lil hungry niggas," Jabari said, pointing and laughing. The other kids and some of the girls laughed too. The girls' counselors were way more organized—they served the girls equal portions; they even said their grace. Camp had started making me notice the girls. Like, really notice them. Some had maple-colored eyes, slanted eyes, shiny smooth skin; some were tall, some short; zigzag cornrows, box braids, afro puffs, French rolls, barrel curls; small Nikes, booty shorts, wide smiles. I watched how they laughed and enjoyed their hefty plates. Twan and me didn't have time to wallow in shame, we had to find food.

We bolted across the room to the cereal stand, yanking at mini boxes of Raisin Bran and Cheerios. "Any milk around here, Unk?" I asked an old slick-face kitchen worker with gold on every tooth.

"Not today, lil buddy. Y'all still hungry after that godly spread?"

He didn't know that we were muscled out of our breakfast by the greedy-ass camp counselor, the person who was supposed to be our leader and who ate enough for five kids, maybe ten—and that his minions did the same. But Twan and I knew that our only choice was to remain silent and eat dry cereal. The one thing we had in common—as east and west Baltimore kids from two completely different worlds— was that snitching wasn't an option.

When Jabari called Twan over for his scraps, Twan collected his plate and looked at me. I know he felt bad for me. He wanted to ask if I wanted some, but he was too scared. That would show weakness: compassion, empathy. What if Jabari and the other kids saw that? So he said nothing.

I wasn't about to take another person's scraps anyway. So I sat there and crunched my dry Raisin Bran until it caked up in my mouth like thick paste, before I washed it down with fountain water.

———

"Young man," a grandma-looking lady said to me, "I need your help with some boxes young man, now, please." I was ducked off in the woods during a game of Hide-and-Go-Seek. We had already gone swimming, played basketball, jumped back in the pool with our basketball clothes on, and mixed in with the girls shuffling Uno cards in the shade to talk them into playing Red Light Green Light, Hot Butter Bean, and Hide-and-Go-Seek in the woods. Hide-and-Go-Seek in the woods was way better than Hide-and-Go-Seek on my block or the projects. The projects were a close second because of the stairwells, I could dip into someone's unit, but the woods provided infinite places to hide and then pop up from behind a tree stump to really scare the shit out of somebody. We had thirty kids playing, my sneakers were covered with specks of mud from running through the woods, but I was fully in the game.

"Young man, come over here!" the woman said again. Her voice was urgent, so I agreed to help her. Strands of her silver hair peeked out of her head wrap, and it matched her shirt with Afrocentric prints. She clutched a mahogany cane with veiny caramel hands, flush with rings and overlapping bracelets. A petite pair of reading glasses floated above her small nose. She led me to a stack of brown boxes. They weren't that big, so I grabbed two at a time. "The shorter way to do many things is to only do one thing at a time. Mozart said that, do you know who that is?" she asked.

I stopped. "No."

I had never seen an older woman dressed with so many rings and necklaces—most of the elderly women from my block just wore their work uniforms with matching lanyards or flowery printed house coats and $1 slippers unless they were getting done up for church or the nightclub.

She told me to take the boxes inside and instructed me on how to stack them for her. She was frying fish while I did it. After I finished, she had a big cup of ice water waiting for me. I downed it in a gulp and asked for some more.

"Thank you, young man. Are you hungry?" she asked. Before I could answer, she continued, "Little boys are always hungry. Follow me to the kitchen, baby, let me get some food in your belly."

I followed the aroma.

"What is your name, darling?"

"They call me D."

"Your actual name," she said, spinning around with a raised eyebrow. "I have no interest in what 'they' call you, sweethcart."

"Dwight, ma'am. Dwight."

She told me that she worked for the camp, and how much she loved the outdoors. "God is nature and nature is God." She then prepared a plate of heaven for me—fried fish, two slices of white bread and a side of butter, a scoop of macaroni salad, Utz potato chips, and a handful of little lobsters.

"I never had little lobsters before, how you eat them?" I asked, jamming fish into my mouth, burning my fingers.

She laughed, plucking the baby lobsters off of my plate. "Darling, you're so cute, these are not lobsters, they're crayfish."

I didn't know how to feel about all the "darlings" and "babies" she gave me. Women in my family didn't talk to me like that. They were harder. We didn't hug, or touch much. I was really never called cute or even handsome. She spoke as if I was special—I never felt special before, I liked it. I didn't know how to show her that I liked it. I wanted to tell her that she was great and I'd check on her every day just to see if she need anything, but I said nothing.

She explained that crayfish are in the same family as lobsters, and that they call them crawfish in the South. She plucked small pieces of meat out of the shell, dabbed it into the butter, and placed it back on to my plate. "There's a creek out back full of them. If you like them, catch them, bring them to me live, and I'll make them for you."

Salty. Spicy. "I like these a lot!" I said.

She plucked more meat out of the crayfish shells and placed them into a pile in front of me. I ate as quick as she loaded my plate, until every single last one of them was gone.

"Young man, have you accepted Jesus into your life?"

"I dunno," I said, sopping the meat with butter and finishing my last piece of fish. "I guess I never really thought about it."

"How old are you? Eleven? Twelve?"

"Nine."

"Nine, darling! A baby!" she said, extending her hands, reaching for mine. "Come to me honey! Come."

I wiped the butter off of my hands and mouth onto my shirt and reached out.

"Bow your head and close your eyes," she said. "Now repeat after me. 'I, Dwight, am a sinner, Lord. I believe You died for my sins, Lord. Right now, I turn from my sins, Lord, and open the door of my heart and life, Lord. I confess You as my personal Lord and Savior.'"

I repeated after her, word for word. She said, "Amen," and I did too.

"Did you feel the spirit?" she asked.

"Yes, I did," I lied. "It's in me, the spirit is in me."

"Well, Dwight," she continued, reaching for a Bible, "you are now protected, you are saved, remember to love your enemies! Pray for those who persecute you! In that way, you will be acting as a true child of your Father in heaven. For He gives His sunlight to both the evil and the good, and He sends rain on the just and the unjust alike. That's Matthew 5:45."

"I won't forget," I said as I made my way out.

"Wake up! Wake up!" Heavy yelled, yanking the covers off of me. I'd had a long day and plenty of crayfish, so I was dozed off, lost in dreamland on my cot. From the force of his pull, I landed on the floor.

"East Side! Get ya lil ass up!" Heavy yelled. It was midway through my first week. A storm had swept through the camp and we were resting in the cabin before dinner. A thick restless energy filled the air—shaken up with the funk of teenage underarms, toes, and corn chip breath that hung in the air. Kareem, who obviously had just been fighting, was pacing, holding his right hand over his eye. "I'ma fuck yo bitch ass up!" he said repeatedly to himself.

"East Side, stand over there!" summoned Heavy, pointing to the corner by the door.

What in the fuck is happening? I thought, following Heavy's orders. I cut through the funk and chorus of screaming boys and made my way to the other side of the room.

"Twan, you ready, Champ? Get over here!" Heavy ordered.

"Yeah, he ready, nigga, you know where we from!" Jabari shouted, pushing Twan into the center of the floor. He was shirtless and frail, deflated even. Sadness covered his face as the boys screamed in his direction.

"East Side, you fightin' tonight, lil nigga!" Heavy breathed, wiping sweat off of his brow. "And if you can't beat Twan, then you gotta get the fuck outta this cabin."

"Twan my friend," I cried. "Man, I don't wanna fight him." I pushed back, terrified. Not scared of fighting Twan, but what was going to happen after that. I'd seen this trick a thousand times, my friends and I pulled this trick—we'd throw a rival kid an easy win against one of our weak friends just so we could have a reason to stomp someone out.

"If you don't fight Twan, you gotta fight Jabari!" Heavy yelled, his face wiggling.

"Fight me, bitch, fuck you!" Twan's high-pitched voice screeched. Jabari and Kareem encouraged him, fueling his ego with verbal poison. "Come on, nigga! Kill that nigga! Fuck the whole east Baltimore!"

Please, Twan, don't do this, please, please don't—I thought, I felt.

I locked eyes with Twan—shirtless, his bird chest poked out, every rib on his torso peeking through his skin, as thin as a quail's wishbone, his back straight, tiny fists attempting to cover his face. His small knees were knocked, feet stepping right, then left, then right again.

I didn't know what got into him, he was the only friend I had made since camp started.

"East Side, is you a bitch?" Kareem spat, still holding his eye. "Huh? Is you a bitch, nigga?"

Two years prior, I had gotten into an argument with my older cousin. We tussled, he slung me to the ground and then spat in my face.

Defeated, I got up and ran toward my house, spit and tears oozing down my jaw. My dad caught me as I turned the corner onto my block, asking me what was wrong. I told him.

Dad's big yellow fist balled up, his face tightened, and he said, "If you run now, you'll be running forever. Go back and punch him in the fucking mouth!"

And that's exactly what I did. I wiped off my face, found my cousin, and punched him in the eye in front of everybody. He then whipped my ass for about ten minutes. It was a really long time to be stomped by shell-toe Adidas. But it felt good that I didn't run or cower. I felt like somebody, and from that day on I fought—I won some and lost some, but I never ran again.

Standing in front of Twan I'd had two years of training—fighting, getting the shit kicked out of me, black eyes, gashes, and bites. Fights and pain were normal. I took it. I didn't cry, I didn't complain afterward. I didn't know if Twan had been through the same, but why was he moving from left to right like a dumbass? Why was his chin exposed, why did he look sad, scared? It's like he never fought before.

The boys formed a circle, making a mini ring in the cabin. Heavy dragged me into the center. "You lose, East Side, I'm gonna take you out back and pour that whole bucket of piss on ya." He laughed, his beady red eyes rolling to the back of his head.

I squared up, placed my feet shoulder width apart—arms balanced, balled hands in front of my face, chin ducked so low it almost touched my neck. My eyes locked in on Twan. He swung a wide left haymaker with his eyes closed. *Twan, man, come on, why do you want to do this?* And he swung again and again, connecting all three times— "Ohhhhhh"s and "Ahhhhhh"s filled the room. His hits didn't hurt at all, not even a little—and I swear I didn't want to hurt Twan, but it was him or me. He swung his fist at me again; this time, I caught his arm and used the momentum of the swing to throw him onto the ground. Easy.

"Come on, man," I said. "Chill, Twan, it's over."

Twan's silent face clearly said that he didn't want to get up, and I knew he didn't because it doesn't take that long to gather yourself from a fall—especially when the adrenaline is rushing.

"Get up and fuck his ass up!" Jabari screamed over everyone.

Twan rose to his feet, same poor stance, same poor look hanging from his face. He swung that same left haymaker, missed, and again with the right, missed, leaving his whole jaw open. I unloaded, maybe five, maybe seven, maybe twenty, but it felt like a thousand blows all on top of his bird face, nose, small teeth, lips, gumline, and on the side of his tiny head. Twan cried, real tears, embarrassing himself and all of the people cheering for him in the room.

"Get up, you faggy bitch!" laughed Heavy, breathing hard like he just fought. He took his Pepsi bottle and poured it all over Twan. "East Side really fucked ya dumb ass up and you goin' pay! Don't think you ain't goin' pay!"

I extended my arm toward Twan. "You good, man?"

Jabari slapped it away. "Don't think you tough now, whore!"

"What? I was—" Jabari sucker-punched me in my mouth, cracking my tooth. I ate it, and fell back into my stance. I squared my feet again, both fists hovering around my face, as salty blood, saliva, and sweat dripped into my mouth. I swallowed it all, and swung a stiff right as he rushed me, and it connected. I cracked him again, but it wasn't strong enough—he was too big. We both fell, me under his weight. I squirmed and wiggled, trying to break free, but to no avail, he was too strong. With his forearm buried in my neck, he used his other fist to pound on my jaw, beat welts into my face, and then took my head and smashed it into the planks of the floor.

"Yoooooo, chill, chill," Heavy said, pulling him off of me. "Chill! Who gonna fight next?"

I made my way to my bed, sucking up my blood in my mouth and dabbing it with my T-shirt.

"East Side, you owe me one, he was gonna kill you!" Heavy breathed across the room. He turned back to the others. "Who gonna fight next? Who?!"

I sat scraping the caked-up mud from the sole of my Jordans onto a small pile of dust on the cabin floor. I had put some twigs I found in the woods in my pocket. I laid them down next to one another and found one that was perfect for the grooves on the soles of my sneakers.

Most of the cabin was still asleep. Evidence of last night's brawl was spread all over the room—torn shirts, dirty socks, cracked chairs, and crushed Pepsi cans.

I angled my Jordans toward the sun and picked the dirt while everyone slept. Michael Jordan's Air Jordans were always clean and pristine when he played—even when Isaiah Thomas and Dennis Rodman and Bill Laimbeer and John Salley of the Pistons collectively got together and cracked the shit out of him, his sneakers still looked untouched. Whether gliding over the Celtics or running straight through the Knicks, Jordan always prevailed. *Men prevail.*

Slowly the boys began to wake and yawn and stretch.

"You alright wit me, lil East Side," Jabari said, extending his hand on his way to the showers. I silently accepted it.

I wanted to punch him right in the teeth. But I knew better. I knew not to do or say anything.

In the bathroom, I looked in the mirror, staring at the dried blood that had sealed the new gash on my face. My front tooth was chipped and tinted by the blood. I rubbed toothpaste on my finger because I hadn't brought a toothbrush. There had been points at camp where I'd thought, *Maybe Mom was right.* When I got home, I'd tell her that I had fun. I'd tell her that I played games in the woods, went swimming, and played basketball. Looking at my face in the mirror, I knew I'd give her the catalogue version that she read about. I'd lie for her.

"I'm gonna go shit!" Heavy announced, as soon as we walked back into the cabin from the showers. "Clean all of this up by the time I get back, then we can eat!"

We pieced together most of the damage and prepared to head over to the hall for breakfast. I didn't fight for a good space in line anymore, there was no point. Heavy and them older dudes weren't sharing any cooked food and I was getting used to my dry cereal in the morning.

As I cracked open my mini box of Raisin Bran, Heavy approached me with a slippery grin, still breathing like he'd run a marathon. "I'ma let you stay in the cabin, lil East Side, but you gotta do sumtin' for my lil homegirl later. She from 'round da way."

What could I do for one of his homegirls? And why does he keep fucking with me? Jabari beating me up wasn't enough—because it didn't break me and Heavy didn't understand why, he just knew that he didn't like me. Maybe it was because I was a kid and already almost as tall as him, or because I wore Jordans and he wore wide-bent shell-toe Adidas with the innards exposed. He often eyed my sneakers the same way I

had Ant's when I first laid eyes on his Jordans. The only difference was that I had them and clearly he couldn't afford them.
He'd probably try to take them if we wore the same size.

I agreed to do whatever Heavy was asking me to do, though
I didn't know what it was, and walked off.

"Yo, Twan, what's up?" I said. He was sitting by himself on
the basketball court. As I inched closer, I heard him weeping,
his face soaked in tears. "What's wrong?"

"They keep calling me faggot," he moaned. "I'm not a
faggot, I'm not a faggot, I'm not."

I sat down next to him. I told him not to worry because we'd
be home soon, and wouldn't have to even think about this
camp anymore. Twan wiped his eyes. "I don't want camp to
end," he said, looking at me. "This is the best part of summer,
I waited all year for this. I don't want to be home."

He said that his stepdad gets drunk, and then gets crazy,
and beats on him and calls him "faggot," too. He showed
me a silver-dollar-sized gash on his arm and another on
his shoulder, both done by his drunk stepdad. Camp was
supposed to be fun.

"You gotta muva and a grandmuva, right?" I asked.

"Yeah, a grandma," he said. "I haven't seen my mother
since she started fuckin' with the crack again. It's been a
month, I think she gone. You gotta dad?"

"Yeah," I said. "He really cool most of the time. I know he
gets high with my uncle, and thinks I don't know. But I know.
And I honestly don't know what's going to happen to him. I
love my dad, and I know somethin' ain't right, because he
would've never let me come here if everything was right."

You wouldn't be able to tell that my dad was getting
high if you didn't know him when he was sober. My dad
wasn't raggedy and toothless like many of the addicts in

the neighborhood. Dad was always clean and well put together—his sweatsuits matched his sneakers, he had nice jewelry, and always a fresh hat that tied everything together. His yellow skin was clear to perfection, and he could've been a model if modeling agencies recruited in places like east Baltimore. The high version of my dad had the same natural swag as the sober version; however, high Dad had moist beige eyes, slurred speech, and pale skin. I also knew he was on drugs, because he never would've dropped me off at that camp.

"Yo, East Side!" Heavy breathed in my direction. "Leave that faggot Twan alone, it's time for you to come with us to the girl cabins. You on tonight."

———————

It was only minutes but the walk to her cabin felt like some hours.

We made it—and I was there, inside the room. She was touching herself and touching me. She guided my hand to her lower thigh, then led it up toward the center where her legs met. She was warm and even more sticky there. Her smell mixed into my skin and now it was sitting in my fingernails. She let my hand go, I yanked it away.

"Nigga, is you scared?" she asked, losing patience. "Where ya rhythm? Ain't you ever finger a girl before?"

"Ummm, yeah, I did, I did," I lied. She shot a big look of disapproval at me. "I finger pop my girlfriend every day."

"You eat her pussy too?" She smiled.

"Nah, I never did nothing like that before," I replied, wiping my hands, her smell, onto my shirt. I knew that was something that the older guys didn't do. But I did have a girlfriend named Konji. She was my age. We played Super Mario, and ate red frozen cups, and we were both terrified of A *Nightmare on Elm Street*. We kissed, without tongue. We made fun of our grandmas' religious rants, our junkie uncles, and talked about how we'd move out of Baltimore. My girlfriend was just like me—there were no long titties, body odors, glitter, glued-on hair weave extensions, vagina rubbing, or dick pulling.

This woman…I didn't know her name. Heavy just kept calling her his *homegirl*, and she never asked my name. Her legs were spread wide. She took some pillows and formed a small fortress on the back of the bed for comfort, and angled herself in my direction.

"Lick all up on here and around here," she ordered, her chin pressed against her neck, holding her panties to the side with one hand and pointing at the folds of her vagina with the other.

I inched toward her, and she pushed the back of my head and buried it deep into her, with more orders. "Move your tongue in a circle, make circles, stick it in there, lick it, boy, lick, lick, lick, lick, boy, lick!"

She yanked her panties until they ripped, firmly wrapped both hands in a cuff around my skull, pulled me even deeper, and ground my lip against all of her folds. I could hardly breathe—my nose and her stink were becoming one. As her grip eased up off of my head she moaned, "Wooooooooo!" and grabbed my fade, digging me in deeper, moving it around with her arm in the directions she wanted it to go in, until she let me go.

She wiped her crotch with her hand and smeared her sticky fluids across my face. "Damn eyelashes, look how wet it is, you wanna stick it in?"

I took a breath, mouth tart, slimy, chin wet, dripping—
and I ran out of there. I ran and ran for a long time, my heart
beating. Someone yelled, "Ay, lil East Side!" but I didn't
stop or turn around—I kept running, outpacing the thumps
in my chest, my tears flying into my ears, past the pool, the
cabin and piss bucket, and straight into the showers that were
forbidden at night. I washed my mouth with water and clear
brown dispenser soap and drowned my face in water until I
felt it in my nose, until it felt like I was drowning.

And when I couldn't smell her anymore, I looked in the
mirror and cried, slowly pulling out each and every one of
my girly eyelashes.

Biting my lip, still smelling a whiff of her stench on my
face, I pulled my T-shirt over my head, wiped the snot and
tears away, and washed my dick with a paper towel. After two
rounds of washing, I slowly made my way back down to camp
where the rest of the boys were.

In the morning I walked into the dining hall and headed
toward the dry cereal.

"Yo, lil East Side, get over here!" Jabari yelled, wrapping his
arm around my neck and rubbing my head. "My lil nigga!"

"Kareem, Jabari, and East Side did their thing last night!"
Heavy yelled, grabbing a handful of French toast sticks, plac-
ing them on a plate, and handing it to me. "Proud of you,
Shorty, what was that pussy like?"

"Oh, man," I said, grabbing the plate, adding syrup, tasting
the warm, buttery, crunchy French toast. "She was wild, boy!
Let me tell you how I got her! What I did to her!"

And then I proceeded to lie.

———

The bus ride home felt quicker—the turns, the beltways, the exit signs were exciting as I felt myself getting closer to home. Most of the kids on my bus had their heads stuck to the window or rested on the shoulder of the person who sat next to them. Everyone was tired, tanned, and the fresh braids that the girls had two weeks ago were now fuzzy, our clothes all dingy, and my sneakers had a brown tint.

I tried to sleep too, but I couldn't, I had one thing on my mind—AIDS. It was a wild thought for a nine-year-old, but it was my first sexual experience, and with a stranger. I couldn't stop thinking about AIDS. My mom worked as a phlebotomist at Johns Hopkins Hospital and would share terrifying stories with me, my sister Mo, and our cousins. "AIDS kills everybody quickly, but if you live, you will have to take sixty pills a day and all of your hair will fall out and some of your skin will fall off and you'd defecate forty-five times a day. Do y'all even know what 'defecate' means?" We didn't but it didn't sound good. It was the '80s, the disease was new and killing Black people at alarming rates, and three of our family members had contracted HIV from intravenous drug use. We heard the adults whisper about Baltimore being known as a hub for AIDS, HIV, and many other sexually transmitted infections, and Mom interacted with the disease every day. We fearfully hung on her every word, and to really nail it to us boys, she'd end with statements like, "And all these little girls have it, they look like you, so you can't tell. If you kiss them or have sex, you will get it too."

I just knew I had AIDS—the woman in the cabin said she had a man, and he probably had a ton of other women who probably had AIDS too, I thought. I felt sick. Did death hurt? I wondered about my mortality. When I was six, there was a man on the basketball court busting dance moves, doing the running man backwards and talking loud. And then he was shot—it all happened in an instant. One second he overflowed with life, and then a gun said, "Pop! Pop! Pop!" and he was gone. I saw the shooter's back as he fled, his big tee filled with air like a parachute. The basketball player just stared toward heaven, mouth and eyes open. He didn't make a sound, it was fast, it couldn't have hurt. If I had to go, I wanted to go fast like him. What brought me back to life was when I saw Dad; seeing him instantly erased any thoughts I had about having AIDS or dying. He always gave me hope no matter the circumstances, he was my strength.

Dad was in a paisley shirt with pants to match and had a fresh cut when the bus pulled up in front of the church. His pants were perfectly creased, shirt neatly tucked, and he wore a big smile, waving to me. I was home. My heart raced, and I shook with excitement as we parked in front of the church. *Let me off of this bus*, I thought. We jumped off of the bus and spread all over the concrete—a forest of dry Jheri curls, Pro Styl gelled fingered waves, trucker hats. Some kids said their goodbyes. "That was fun, yo's!" I squeezed past them with my bag. I couldn't wait to get back to my friends, my block, my sneakers, my life. "Lil East Side!" Heavy yelled, pulling me in for one last nasty embrace. "This was my lil brother, he a tough one! You coming back next summa?"

"Prolly, I'll catch y'all later!" I lied, pulling away, running to my dad. I knew Dad could overhear Heavy—witnessing the respect that I earned from all of the counselors and kids alike, and he was welling up with joy. He looked pleased, like when his scratch-offs or numbers hit. He was happy that I held my own. I ran toward him, and when I reached him,

I held him. I sunk my face and my tears into his paisley, and just let them flow.

"Come on, let's get in the car," Dad said.

I pulled my T-shirt over my head, soaking up the rest of the tears. And as soon as I got in the car, Dad looked at me and said, "Are you okay?"

I continued to wipe away tears.

————

"So, how was it?" my father asked as we drove home. His face was bent, eyes wet slits, with tears creeping out and sliding down both of his cheeks. I could tell he was clean now. "You toast marshmallows and go hiking like *Leave It to Beaver*?"

"Who? You mean, was the homie Lil Beaver from Greenmount Avenue there?"

"Nigga, what?! It's an old show, boy," Dad said, laughing.

"Camp was alright. It was cool," I lied. "I learned how to catch and eat crayfish. They taste like crabs a little bit."

I couldn't tell him what happened with the woman in the pink skirt, or with Heavy. He couldn't save me; it was over now. No one could save me. I could only save myself, decide to win or lose. I chose to win.

It was the wrong side to choose.

BOOK II

a dad story

5–13 years old, 1985–1993

Like most of the street kids from my
generation, I was born with two dads.

1

The first dad I had was biological, the loving guy who had no idea of how horrible the camp that he dropped me off to attend was: Dwight Watkins, also known as Big Dwight (because I'm Lil Dwight), Jump (because he jumped a lot as a baby), Polite Dwight, or Reds (a nickname for all fair-skinned men); he could also be called the name of whatever high yellow dude was most famous at the time—Al B. Sure!, any member of DeBarge, Christopher Williams, Redman, and the list goes on.

I was always Lil Dwight or Lil D in our tiny section of east Baltimore, a moniker that I proudly wore in his shadow.

Being his son was an honor. Dad wasn't the richest or the *flyest*, but he was present. During the crack era, when crack, crack sales, and prison ate up the other dads in my neighborhood, mine was still around living and breathing in my house. My friends all longed for their fathers, but most of them were either dead, addicted, or missing. Big Dwight was synonymous with partying, dance moves, laughs, new sneakers, working in the processing department of Good Samaritan Hospital, or performing one of his thousand side hustles, spending that money as soon as it touched his pocket, and always, always having a good time—you always knew when he was around, because the angriest people would begin to smile.

My other father was the streets. I belonged to my block, the alleys and busted-up avenue corners that outlined my life. The boarded-up row houses with plywood windows and yellow WARNING tape made me.

Funny thing about the streets is that they were just like my blood father—sometimes everything I needed and other times the root of my problems.

When I was with Big Dwight, I got to be a boy. With the streets, I had to be a man. I had to think, act, and respond quickly. When blood fathers fall short or aren't around, the streets compensate.

On payday, you'd catch Big Dwight smiling, frying something, belting out lyrics as loud as possible over the music blaring from his speakers. I'd get home, see him leaning on the stove whipping up mayonnaise-heavy seafood salad with too *too* much imitation crab meat. He'd be mad I was out late, or talked too much about the block, and yell, "Boy, the streets will never love you!" Dad was raised by the streets too. He was a product of the block. The same pavement that I was a product of.

I didn't see what his issue was. The streets had created his style, his language, and taught him those dance moves. It had fathered him too. His manhood was measured and vetted by the streets.

I hated when OGs told me things like that, or said, "Don't sell drugs." Even though the same OG made a ton of money and lived like a fucking star. Then he ended up being shot, letting his family down and doing a prison bid, but that story doesn't push a kid away from the streets. It makes our hold on it even tighter. Going to jail, being shot, and letting down our families is always worth the reward of living like a fucking star—like roses, so beautiful to have them, we endure the pricks from their thorns. It's candy to us Black boys, a syrupy red poison that we can't wait to drink up. The kind that's addictive and always makes you smile. In search of that juice, I armed myself with the tales I heard from Dad, or my big brother and older cousins, or the uncles and everyone else who took on the streets and lost. I was going for it, foolishly I was ready to get in a game that has had some wins, but never, ever any real winners.

———

"The more you cry," Dad said, "the less you piss!"

"KINDERGARTEN" was written in big colorful letters neatly arranged in an arc over the door.

I wiped my face, smeared the tears until they dried.

It was the first day—the first day ever spending time with complete strangers. My babysitter Boo Boo and her mom, Miss Tookie, had been my daily routine when Mom left for work. They'd sip bitter Maxwell House coffee and give me sips in between my begging and grease my flaky scalp every day for as long as I could remember.

This place was…cold, sterile.

"Boy, wipe ya face off!" Dad said. "Come here."

One of his hands gripped my tiny afro, angling my head toward the sun, the other hand extending his pointer finger toward my nostril. He dug, dug, dug. "Stay still! Dirty-ass nose!"

I hate this. I hate this. I hate this.

Now my tears were enough to flood my face. The teacher was looking. Dad kept digging. His finger would never fit, could never fit. He dabbed it with a glob of spit, and scratched away any remaining morning crud from my lips and the corners of my eyes, added more spit, and then smoothed out my eyebrows.

"You look clean now. No more crying. Go in there and take care of business." He patted me on the head. "Do what you gotta do. No crying."

———

Dad and I sat on the bench inside of the hood's favorite sneaker store, Charley Rudo's sports in Mondawmin Mall. I peeled off my old white Adidas and slid on a pair of brand-new Nike Air Force 1s. I laced them up tight, strapped them, and took a few leaps, feeling my feet bond with the cushion and Air technology for the first time. "Yeah, they fit!" I said.

"Lil man, you gonna wear them out the store?" asked Clarence, who was the shoe salesman and also my father's homeboy.

"I think I only wear Nike now," I giggled like a fat kid in a Hershey factory, examining the bright white leather and metallic silver swoosh.

"Throw them old shoes away, boy!" Dad said, shuffling cash in his hands, and then passing it to Clarence.

"Thanks, Jump," Clarence said, glancing over his shoulder, sliding the cash into his pocket instead of ringing us up at the cash register. He walked the new Nike box with my old shoes into the back of the store. This was clearly a hustle for both of them, Dad paying below retail and Clarence making 100 percent profit on the company's dime, while still getting his hourly wage. I wonder how hard managers flipped out when they finally found all of the old shoes Clarence swapped for new ones.

Dad and I walked out of the mall happy and singing:

We are the world, we are the children
We are the ones who make a brighter day, so let's start
giving...

I kept pausing to look at my shoes—the best shoes I ever owned.

"The novelty always wears off of any materialistic thing," Dad said. "You think you want that shit, but you don't need that shit. They just shoes."

We headed to the bus stop—Dad's car was in the shop. As we reached the bench, clouds flung open like a blasted door and heavy rain poured down on us. Daylight vanished in a blink as the storm grew.

"Shit, we gotta get a hack!" Dad yelled, trying to shield me with his coat. A hack in Baltimore is a cheap unregulated meterless Uber, before Uber was invented—normally driven by an old Black dude in a Kangol hat. A ride either down the street or all the way across town cost $5. But we weren't having any luck catching one. My new Airs sounded floppy and spongy as we looked for cover, but they were still clean; this storm hadn't washed the novelty off. Dad stuck his hand out, signaling at cars, and they all just kept driving by. Ten, twenty, thirty minutes, no hack. He then waved a $20 bill and that didn't work either.

"So look right," Dad said half laughing, half contemplating— he paused to take a sip out of his purple velvet bag. Rain dripping down his face and his hand gripping my shoulder, he looked me squarely in the eyes. "Act like you crying."

"What?" I screamed, over the wind, the rain. "I won't cry! Nothin' can make me cry!"

"Good, but act like it!" he laughed, taking another sip. "That's the only way we gonna get a ride and out of this damn rain!"

I put my head down, forced out my giggles at his request, and then balled my face tight and rubbed my eyes, as if the storm was the worst thing that ever happened to me. Dad kneeled down, putting an arm around me, rocking me like a baby. Everything was going to be okay.

"Waaaaaaaah! Waaaaaaaah!" I let out one ugly wet yelp after another. I screamed so loud, and was so deep into the con, that even I started believing I was sad.

"My God, are you homeless?" a big-haired, extra blonde white woman shouted from a long black town car. "Please get in, please! Hurry!"

"We good now, stop crying, nigga," Dad snickered, slipping the wet $20 back into his pocket, ushering me into the back of the car.

2

Dad held the door open with one hand, allowing me to walk first into the cloudy two-bedroom unit. Lanky black silhouettes floated in and out of the bedroom, delivering handshakes, high fives, and a barrage of "Hey Lil D," "Aye Lil Dwight." We were supposed to be headed to the circus the next day, and I needed to keep an eye on him, to make sure he wasn't out too late or didn't drink too much, or whatever else could have happened to mess up our plans. I had been seeing the Ringling Bros. and Barnum & Bailey commercials on television all week— the elephants, the monkeys, the flying acrobats, the magic. It was the best shit I ever saw in my life, and I never knew a person that had attended a real circus before. This was my chance, we could be the first to witness the glory of Ringling Bros. and Barnum & Bailey. I just had to go.

"Go in that room with the rest of the little bastards," Dad said, his gold tooth gleaming in the dim light. He pointed to the other bedroom down the hall, on the other side of the apartment. "I'll call you when I'm ready."

I walked down the hall, stepping over soiled clothes, toys, and other items scattered across the floor. Inside the room, there were a bunch of kids, eight-, nine-, and ten-year-old boys, piled up in front of a huge thirty-inch color TV. "Huge" because the little round bubble screen was encased in the center of about eighty pounds of wood that stood taller than us. Our dark skin was wrapped in the blue TV light. It was my homie Fat Nick's house, and his mom's bedroom held one of the nicest big screens in the neighborhood, the best I'd ever seen. They were playing Mike Tyson's Punch Out!! game.

"Gimme the joystick, bitch!" my cousin Bunk yelled at Nick. "It's my go!" I found an empty space on the bed next to him.

Bunk grabbed Nick's plump neck and squeezed hard enough where we could see swirly welts coming through his skin. And then Bunk cuffed his teeth, dragged Nick across the floor, and pried the joystick out of his hands. Nick rushed back at him, but Bunk knocked him back. Nick threw an Etch A Sketch at his head. Bunk picked it back up and started to beat Nick with it. I had to stop it. "Yo, that's enough!" I said, pinning Bunk against the wall. "They gonna make us cut the game off."

Nick wanted a second chance because he'd lost to Glass Joe, the weakest character on the game. He probably should've gotten a second chance because we were in his house, in his mom's bedroom, playing his Nintendo—but it was Bunk's turn and he was far from the weakest person in the room. "Give me back the game, I'm not done!" Nick continued. Everyone was laughing.

"Shut the fuck up back there!" one of the grown-ups from the kitchen yelled over the music. We all looked at each other. Sick of being around fighting kids, I leaped off the bed and followed the music and smoke and chicken fumes back down the hallway.

Every Friday night the adults got together in Nick's kitchen for card games—Spades, Tonk, Pinochle, or all three. There was loud music and a lot of smoke, weed, cigarettes, and burned incense. Nick's mom always fried chicken. I can't remember her not frying chicken. Just two minutes or thirty seconds in their apartment and you'd instantly smell like the Colonel, even if you'd bathed in cologne like Dad.

"Game over, fucka!" Dad yelled, leaping up from his folding chair, his voice bouncing off the walls. "Pay me, lil nigga! Pay me!"

Dad was always the biggest personality in a room, even the whole building, even when surrounded by the biggest personalities. He was the loudest, the yellowest, with the biggest smile and biggest laugh—his presence easily touched all four corners of a space as soon as he entered. Everyone else disappeared around my father, but he was never a ham, he didn't try to outshine anyone, he just does.

"Y'all taking all the food out my kids' mouth, I'm gettin' it all back!" he yelled, laughing, smiling, sitting right at the center of the table. "You better come eat some of this burnt-ass chicken, Lil Dwight, this might be ya last meal in a while, if I don't make this money back."

The party table shook with laughter.

"I don't want no fuckin' chicken," I said. The table laughed more. Grown-ups loved me cursing, they thought it was the funniest thing in the world. "Fuck that chicken!"

"Don't cuss at me, you little motherfucker," Dad yelled back over the laughter.

"Make a plate!" Dad said, shuffling his cards, "We ain't stoppin' to get food if ya little ass get hungry later on!"

I grabbed Cheetos out of a flowery bowl and dumped them onto a paper towel. I was licking the orange dust off of my fingers when my uncle Angelo, also known as Big Lo, sprang from the living room. "Watch out!" He put me into a headlock on the couch.

He stood up and playfully started bobbing and weaving to show me how to put up my guard. "Stay ready!"

I faced him, tiny hands protecting my face, and he quickly poked at my ribs. "You better be ready for the court!" He always said that. With glossy eyes and a ball cap, he started to throw imaginary crossovers and perfect his hook-shot form. I pretended to block his shots.

"Man, y'all take that goofy basketball shit outside!" Dad yelled from the card game.

"You got any little girlfriends yet?" Big Lo asked.

"Yeah, I got two! They both like me!"

He laughed and gave me a high five. "Two ain't enough, you should have four!"

"Already a lil heartbreaker, justtttttttt like his faaa-tha!" a woman with a round smile from the card game said through the smoke.

He was a tough act to follow, but I tried. Dad was handsome by definition. Women and even little girls my age loved him. At five foot ten, he was stylish and generously poured into everyone around him, sharing his money, his time, and his liquor. Everywhere we went, everyone loved him.

"You better make sure you can keep them all happy," Dad chuckled.

When Dad was drunk his loud mouth was even louder, his eyes were sleepy, and he laughed so hard that I wanted a sip. I wanted to laugh like him. Purple Crown Royal bags were everywhere that he went and could be found all around the house. I kept my money in them, toys; they were my pencil bags for school; they were stuffed in the kitchen drawer like recycled shopping bags, Mom's knick-knacks filled some of them, my cousins' fingernail polish, Dad had one full of rubbers—basically it felt like everybody in our family had unlimited Crown Royal bags because of Dad and my uncles. Crown Royal was like Red Rooster hot sauce, Newport cigarettes, and petroleum jelly—they were in everybody's house.

"Jump been losing all night," Clarence said, looking over his huge glasses, adjusting his Kangol and shaking his head. "Y'all ain't going to no fuckin' circus! He probably gonna be headed home with no shoes on. You gonna loan your dad some money?"

"I won't need a loan, shit!" Dad said, his cards close to his face. "If I said we are going to the circus, we are going to the motherfuckin' circus!"

A collage of crinkled ones, fives, and twenties were spread across the kitchen table, making a faded green trail around the red cold cups, cigarette-butt-packed ashtrays, and plastic chip bowls.

"Circus money," one of the ladies snickered.

"Deal me in next hand," Big Lo shouted, headed toward the bathroom. "I'm takin' some circus money too!"

Dad had been promising a trip to the circus all week, and now we weren't going? I made myself into a ball on the couch. Their stupid card game meant more to me than it ever had. I watched them shuffle the cards around the table as they yelled, rolled up, snorted, and the sweaty women folded bills into triangles and stuffed them into their bras. They all kept running in and out of the bathroom. Their records never stopped spinning—Aretha Franklin, Frankie Beverly, Luther Vandross, and "Solid as a Rock" over and over again. It felt like their game would go on forever, and it did, until all the smoke weighed on my eyelids and I dozed off.

"Get up!" Dad said, tickling me, as the sun hit my face. "Boy, let's go get you a new sweatsuit and some tennis shoes, we gonna be at the circus all day!"

I opened my eyes to his wide smile. He was holding a stack of money thicker than an AT&T phone book.

3

"550! 550! I've been seeing 550 all day!" I screamed at my dad, busting up his conversation.

He was hanging out on the corner with Big Lo and Clarence. About two months earlier, I picked the winning number. "Dad, I had a dream 357 came out straight," I told him over cereal, but he didn't play it—because he thought I was just messing around. He was so sick of watching 357 flash across the screen that he yelled, "BITCH! SHIT! FUCK!" loud enough to wake the neighbors. Dad told me that if a number ever came to me again, I had better tell him, and if it won, then he was going to pay me.

"Slow down, slow down!" Dad said to me. "Lemme write it down."

He pulled out an open envelope from his back pocket.

"I took a piss this morning and the clock said 5:50 a.m., the new baseball mitt I had to pick up for today's game was on 550 Ellwood Avenue at the assistant coach's house," I explained. He kneeled down next to me and jotted down the number next to a bunch of other numbers. "550 was scribbled on the box my coach had pulled the glove out, and then the case where all of our mitts were stored said something about 550 dollars. 550, Dad, 550!"

"I got it, I got it, play 550! What time is your baseball game?" he asked.

"We play at two o'clock."

"Okay, cool, I'll see you after I put this and the rest of my lotto numbers in."

Dad wasn't into sports. He'd only attended one of my baseball games, where I embarrassed myself and my entire team. I was squared on the plate with two strikes and a foul, when the pitcher hummed a wild curveball in my direction that soared dead center over the plate. "STRIKE!" the umpire yelled. The catcher missed the ball on my third strike, which meant that I had the right to haul ass to first base, and instead of running like I should've, I sat there like a dumbass because I had never heard of the rule. Everyone booed me as I walked back to the bench. I wanted to cry.

Dad never made it to my game, and I'm happy that he didn't. My team won, but not only did I strike out every time I approached the plate, I tackled the pitcher after he pierced my chest with a fastball. I was kicked out of the game.

I walked back to my block to see all the regular neighborhood corner dudes, minus my dad. They were sitting out, rolling weed, bumping music, sipping.

"Y'all see my father?" I asked.

"He probably out spendin' that lotto number, Pick 3 came out," said Big Lo.

The last time Dad hit the number, I got a new pair of Air Jordans and he took us out to eat.

I spent the next few hours looking for Dad. I wanted to know if it was 550 that hit. Then I saw him roll up on the block. "550 straight good job!" he said, smiling. He gave me a proud handshake. There was a $50 bill folded into his palm and he planted it into mine. "I should've put more money on it!" He smirked and I smirked back. "Every time you feel that way about a number, you come get me," he said, and I nodded in agreement. It was a silent commitment.

He walked to his car and pulled off. *Thirty more dollars*, I thought, *and I can grab a pair of Bo Jacksons.*

4

The Exotic Auto Show came to the Baltimore Convention Center every year around February 10, my birthday. And every year I wanted to go, and for my tenth birthday Dad had agreed to take me again. The convention was the birthday gift that kept on giving. This year would be even better, as the commercial on TV boasted about hundreds of new additions, both brand-new and classic models. Dad and I jumped in the car and zipped across town, taking Bunk along. Nick, Bunk, and I had gone together last year. This year Nick was away with his family, so he couldn't make it. It was a good day.

We sat in red Ferraris, posed in Beemers, and took pictures in front of all kinds of foreign automobiles that we couldn't pronounce. When we got back to the block, we walked up my steps, Dad trailing a few feet back, and I opened the door.

"Surprise! Surprise!" yelled my whole family. My siblings, aunts, uncles, cousins, a bunch of friends, and the bulk of my whole block were there. All for me. And it was a real party. The first surprise party I ever had, and they scared the shit out of me, but I was cool and thanked everyone.

I made my way over to the dance floor and blended in while "Poison" by Bell Biv DeVoe pumped out of the speaker.

That girl is poison
Never trust a big butt and smile
That girl is poison poison

I was rocking back and forth, and doing a two-step, when I suddenly locked eyes with La Tesha. She laughed, not at me, but with me. Then I noticed everyone else laughing— looking in my direction. Was my dancing that bad? I checked my sneakers, they were still clean, and my clothes, nobody spilled juice on me. What's so funny? I spun around and there was Dad cutting up the dance floor, his Nikes sliding from left to right, spin moves, dips. The kids formed a circle and "Go Big Dwight! Go Big Dwight! Go!" was chanted for at least ten minutes from fist-pumping kids and their parents. It was so loud and exciting that my uncles joined in. It got so loud that the cops came to ask us to turn down the music, and we did, and when they left, we cranked it again, this time Biz Markie...

You, you got what I need but you say he's just a friend
And you say he's just a friend, oh buby,
You got what I need but you say he's just a friend...

Dad was still dancing, "Disco Dwight," I told La Tesha. "They should call him Disco Dwight."

5

"Yo, my mother and your father some fuckin' junkies," Nick said, his eyes locked on Tecmo Super Bowl.

"My father ain't no junkie," I spit back. "Fuck outta here, boy!"

My mind went to the hypodermic needles on the curb in front of our door, in the kitchen, stuffed in the purple Crown Royal bags hidden in the closet and on top of the medicine cabinet and in shoeboxes and out back by the trash. I had been finding them for weeks. Hypodermic needles were clear with black lines on the side that captured the measurements, the tips were orange, and they were always empty and uncapped when I found them.

"Bum-ass niggas, fuckin' losers," Nick said. He inflated his round cheeks and blew a hot Cheeto breath as I drowned him out, laying back on the box spring, watching my dusty ceiling fan rotate. *Junkies*, I thought.

In our neighborhood, an addict, or what everyone called a "junkie," was the worst label to have, bottom of the bottom, lowest of the low, a truly fucked-up person. Junkies stole from their spouses, their children, their elderly parents, themselves.

Lately, Dad had been looking like a set of floating clothes—

his empty sweatsuits hung on fragile shoulders. His trademark sun-kissed yellow skin had become as pale as his demeanor. He rarely laughed these days.

The next day I avoided Nick. I was still in my head, still thinking about what he said—still hoping it wasn't true. I sat on my steps for hours with a toothbrush and my custom sneaker solution, scrubbing crud out of the bottom of my Jordan 5s. I thought about how my uncles got high. My father's brothers, they stole. They stressed out the whole family with their rotted brown and yellow teeth. My friends and I laughed at them and their fucked-up gumlines. They were a joke.

Suddenly, Luther Vandross's voice screamed from down the street, "Neva too much! Neva too much!" Its volume made our small block tremble. It was my dad. He parked in front of me and jumped out of the car. He looked like the old him, smaller, but healthy, and was singing over the music, on beat. He was wearing the cheek-raising grin that I loved to see.

"Carry some of this stuff in the house," he told me.

I tossed my Jordans to the side and leaped off of the steps, meeting Dad by the car.

Fuck Nick, I thought.

1:20 a.m.

"BOW!" The door was knocked off the hinges into splinters.

With a headphone cord wrapped around my neck, I darted toward my sister's room. "Yo, what the fuck!" Dad yelled, rushing through his bedroom door. He was half-naked, standing in the hall, while two gunmen darted up to the second level toward us. "Get the fuck back in the room!" one of them shouted at Dad. "Get the fuck in the room!" One of the gunmen ushered all of us into the front bedroom. My sister and I listened as they began digging through our belongings. I saw yellow eyes in a skull cap stomp toward the bedroom. "Who's in here?" he shouted at Dad. "Who else is in here?"

"Shhhhhhh," Dad told us. "It'll be okay."

The other gunman, a shorter guy, with long curly locks, posted up in front of us, his shoulders squared and his gun centered.

"Calm down," he said. "We won't be long."

We sat in the dark, his pistol trained on us, waiting.

"Hey, let my family go," Dad said, eyes wet, slowly standing up. "Just let my family go, take me."

"Sit back, get back!" the gunman said, tightening his grip. "Don't get shot tonight!"

Dad stood in front of us on guard, his arms spread, waiting.

"Ain't shit in here," the gunman rummaging through the living room downstairs said. "The shit ain't in here!"

The gunman in front of us nodded at us. "Don't leave this room or else!"

He then jetted down the steps, and both of them ran out the front door.

Dad ran to the phone and called the cops.

Hours passed.

————

4:30 a.m.

"Your doors are bad," a smug milk-colored cop said, greeting us. "These cheap doors make this house a target."

"So our doors are the reason it took y'all so long to get here?" Dad asked the cop.

"I'm just saying," the cop said.

On the way to the basketball court the next day, I said to Nick, "My father is a fuckin' soldier." We were walking down Fayette Street. "A real hero type." Nick was listening intently and nodding. "He poked his chest out and stood up for us when it mattered." I was happy with Nick's reaction. That's not what *junkies* do.

That's what men do.

6

Don Don was the kind of guy I wanted to be: tall, funny, bright white teeth, with a perfect fade, who could dunk on you backwards with both hands. He was a jump shooter, popular, and the owner of a 300Z T-Top with BBS rims. That summer I split my time between two parks playing ball, Bocek and Ellwood—trailing behind my big cousins Kevin and Darnell, who we called Don Don. He was from the streets, but not really a street guy. Don Don wore clean Air Max, or Huaraches, the track version, with invisible ankle socks. And every time he opened his mouth, funny spilled and we laughed it up. Don Don made us laugh until we literally cried, until our chests ached, until we begged him to stop cracking jokes; he never did and we loved him for it even more. None of these attributes, these qualities I dreamed of having, mattered when he was shot and killed.

A girl he casually dated had a boyfriend that he didn't know about until the day that disgruntled boyfriend approached him. Armed, her boyfriend stood at the bottom of our block, asking, "Who is Don Don?" Don Don didn't want to beef, he wanted to talk it out, to be funny, to ease the guy's spirit, to tell that guy he didn't know she was in a relationship—that he could have her and life could go on. So Don Don made his way toward the bottom of our block, and was met with bullets before they could converse. Bullets rained for twenty seconds, leaving young Black bodies stretched across the concrete. Paralyzed, blood flowing. A few of us wanted to move Don Don out of the street and up onto the sidewalk, but he was dead.

The day after Don Don's murder, large foil-covered trays and buckets of fried chicken, syrupy sweet potatoes, macaroni and cheese, biscuits, muffins, pound cake, all types of cognac and vodka, and a couple of 40s showed up at my aunt's house from family and friends. My big cousins were not new to loss and had figured out many ways to cope — eat, drink, smoke, and snort their pain away. Me, I was posted in the corner, fighting back tears.

"You okay?" Dirty Larry, a family friend, asked me. "You holdin' up?"

"Yeah, I'm straight," I lied, with a stiff shrug.

It was an expression that had been passed down to me, the easiest lie I always told. *I'm straight.*

Dirty Larry reached in for a hug. "It's gonna be okay…"

I yanked away from him. "Nigga, get the fuck off of me, man. Dirty bitch! Is you crazy?"

The whole room of drinking, smoking, and eating cousins laughed hysterically, giving me daps and praise.

"Lil Dwight funny as I don't know what, man!"

"My lil cousin a soldier!"

Dirty Larry, defeated, didn't buck back. He just slumped his shoulders and wandered away to another room, shaking his head.

"Fuck is wrong with that clown?" I said to my older cousins. They nodded and passed me the liquor. I took a swig, it burned slow and left me dizzy as I ate up the validation, like they ate the sweet-potato pie in celebration of Don Don's life.

"What's so funny?" Dad said to the room. "You okay?"

"Dirty Larry tried to hug me, I told him to get off me!"

"That's right!" Dad breathed. "Don't you ever, ever let anybody touch you!"

I nodded. Boys who cried or sought affection were called "faggots" and "bitch-ass niggas." Boys who cried had to stay on the porch. Tough kids beat them, excluded them from games, took their toys and broke them into pieces.

"You holdin' up?" my father asked. "Don Don was a great kid, he deserved better. Are you alright?"

I couldn't say no and show weakness. I was too old now to hug him, or to want to hug him. I couldn't cry on his shoulder or anybody's shoulder. I knew my only option: take the pain, bury it deep inside of myself, and then pour liquor on it, enough to drown it so that it never resurfaced. And then pour even more liquor on it.

"I'm straight, Dad," I lied. "Everything is fine."

BOOK III

a man story

15–20 years old, 1995–2000

"It is easier to build strong children than
to repair broken men."
—Frederick Douglass

Dad walked up on me, pointing the cordless phone in my direction. "Lenny's loudmouth ass is on the phone."

He playfully shoved the phone toward me.

"Yo, we leave at like 7 a.m. from that parking lot by Dunbar Middle!" my homie Lenny yelled into the receiver like he was on a bullhorn.

"Yeah, I know, I know."

"Yo, stay the night at my spot. I got the house to myself," he said. "Mom's on a church trip. We can get up early and be the first ones on the bus in the morning. I want to sit next to Shannon, she thicka than a project cockroach, and you should sit with her sister. She like ya lil ugly box-head ass!"

"Nigga, fuck you."

"Fuck you, box-head, see ya lata!"

I had just enrolled in Dunbar High School, and Lenny had arrived a year before me. We were heading to an amusement park in Virginia called Kings Dominion the next morning, and I had big plans. I'd link up with my upcoming classmates, especially the girls; ride all the rides and load up on funnel cake; and we'd crack jokes during the entire three-hour bus ride there, then sleep all the way back home.

I was debuting my new Air Max 95s. I'd rock them with the top strings undone like my boy JT showed me. "I don't know why, but the girls love when I don't tie my shoes alla way up!" he'd say. "Wear them strings loose, D!"

I hung up and packed my bag for Lenny's. First, I wanted to stop at Nick's crib. My father said that he'd called too, but I was sleeping.

As soon as I entered his apartment, Nick said, "I need a favor, D." His eyes were yellow and paranoid. "I don't ask you for too much, but hol' this hamma for me." He walked around nervously, pulling his Raiders snapback hat on and off, using the brim to scratch his head. The sweet chubby kid I loved to play video games with had turned full gangster. "I'ma get it right back, but I need it gone for at least ova the weekend."

I owed Nick a thousand favors. He always looked out for me, and it didn't matter if I needed his help in a fight or needed extra dollars, Nick always had my back.

"No problem."

Nick passed me a bag. I glanced inside. It was a two-toned .45.

"Yo, chill, man, tuck that thing away, man. And be careful, the safety broke. You know you the only one I trust wit this, man?"

"Don't worry," I said.

This was a no-brainer. I made my way to Lenny's. I'd stash the gun at his house while we went to the amusement park. His mom was never home. She stayed on a church tour, praising Jesus from state to state.

I went straight to the blue couch in his mother's bedroom, removed that annoying layer of plastic that was stuck to the fabric, and tucked the gun deep inside of the cushions. Then I reapplied the plastic.

Lenny said he didn't mind holding the gun. We ordered Chinese food and sat in front of his house until 2 a.m., laughing, joking, calling girls, and eating shrimp fried rice and greasy beef yat gaw mein—we pronounced it "yak-a-me." Lenny could finish a family-size order on his own. He was tall and football husky with an appetite that never quit.

"You gonna finish ya rice?"

"Nah, ain't no more shrimp in there."

"Shidddd, you crazy, lemme have it," Lenny said, swiping my box. "Shid this rice good as a bitch!"

Before bed, I laid out my clothes for the trip across the top of his couch, and noticed how my new white shirt enhanced the texture of my Air Max 95s. I then dozed off to reruns of *Def Comedy Jam*.

POP! POP POP! I jumped up at the sound of gunshots.

Lenny was asleep in another room. I peeked out of the window and saw cop cars swarming the projects. Gunshots and police raids were normal business in my neighborhood, and Lenny's too. It didn't look like anything unusual was happening. I laid down to go back to sleep.

BOOM! The front door blew off the hinges.

"Yoooooo, who the fuck is that!" Lenny yelled from upstairs.

I climbed over the couch to hide, but was yanked up by my neck. Pale white hands flipped me back over the couch and slammed me onto the floor. My face was buried into the carpet, with the hands squeezing my wrists. From the side of my eye, I could see police, so many cops, like the whole department. A cop dragged Lenny down the stairs, his head hitting every step like a rag doll.

Somebody had been murdered—those were the gunshots I'd heard—and a "reliable citizen" had pointed to Lenny's house, or so they said.

"We don't fuck wit drugs!" Lenny yelled. "We play sports!"

"Shut up, bitch!" a cop answered.

We were minors, yet we were taken downtown to Homicide without our parents' consent and held for hours. No food, no phone calls to our parents or anyone else, just questions. They asked us question after question about our whereabouts; who we knew, what we did that day. We didn't know anything and wouldn't have said anything if we did. More questions came our way until the sun started showing its face. I kept thinking about the bus to Kings Dominion. We missed it. We'd been so excited to go on this trip and now we couldn't because we were detained, for something we didn't do, something we knew nothing about. I needed my dad.

When the police freed us, I called Dad first.

"You don't ever talk to them racist muthafuckers!" he spat through the receiver. "Always shut up unless you sayin' 'lawyerrrrrrr!' Stay strong and we can beat them devils!"

"Oh, you know I ain't say a word."

Then he said that he loved me and was picking me up before he went to work.

"Love you too," I said back.

———

I went home and slept the anger off. The gun was the first thing that came to mind when I woke up the next morning, so I threw on some shoes and ran back over to Lenny's.

"You ain't gonna believe this shit, cuz," Lenny said to me from up the block. "All our shit gone!"

Either someone told the rental office about the raid or Lenny's mom hadn't paid their rent. He didn't know, but either way their belongings were put outside the next day. The dirty management company didn't even give his mom a heads-up before they tossed their furniture, clothes, his video games, and all of their belongings all over the street. Crackheads had a field day—free Nikes to sell, free kitchen appliances to sell, free whatever-you-could-carry-without-getting-caught to sell. I ran up to the house out of breath, hands on both knees, chest deflated.

My mind immediately went to the gun. The cops would've kept us if they'd found it. I looked around the house. A blender, dishes, a flipped-over kitchen table, a broken stereo, some clothes, shoes, bras, and no blue couch.

The blue couch was gone. I'd lost the gun.

———

"Is you from da east or west side?" a lighthearted voice said in my direction.

"East," I replied, sitting in class Monday morning, with my head stuck to my desk. The history teacher was talking but I couldn't hear anything. All I could think about was getting Nick's gun back.

"East Baltimore niggas is so dirty!" she said. "You really from over there?"

I lifted up my head and looked at her with a twisted brow like, *Girl, leave me alone.* I had a headache, the kind that pumped and pulsated with every move. If I angled my body the right way, I could direct the pain to a tolerable part of my head and make it through class.

"Girl, you know when east Baltimore niggas is clean cuz they act all stuck-up," she said to her friend. "Your Jordans a lil bit cute, though. Did they just come out?"

"No," I said, briefly picking my head up. "I always buy

two pairs when I can. One to wear and eventually hoop in, and another to pull out for times like this, to confuse people like you."

She laughed, rolling her eyes. I laughed too.

"Oh, okay, you must got money, new boy."

I covered my head with my jacket. I didn't want to bug Lenny about the gun—he had just been through hell with the eviction and all—but Nick had called me at 5 a.m. screaming, "Yo, I need the gun! It's an emergency!"

And now I'm stuck in school with cackling girls, not knowing what to do.

"Mister, ah mister!" the stumpy teacher, dressed in three different shades of JC Penney brown, said, looking at his roll sheet. "Excuse me! Tap him."

"New boy!" she said. "Get up! The teacher callin' you!"

I looked up. "Yeah."

"Since you can't seem to keep your head up, won't you go to the office and explain your problems to them!" he snarled.

"I ain't got a problem" easily rolled off of my tongue as I stood up and walked out of the class.

"I'm going to the bathroom," said the cackling girl, following me out of the room.

In the hallway, she introduced herself. I told her my name is Dwight, but to call me D. She asked me why I was so standoffish.

I laughed, told her she was cute. "I'm not standoffish, I don't know you. But let's leave now so I can get to know you."

She said she had a boyfriend.

I asked her why she was bothering me if she had a boyfriend.

"You know you can be friends with a girl without trying to fuck her, right?" she said.

"For real?" I said. I was serious. I didn't know. It was high school and I had girls as friends, but most of them were lesbians. Everyone else of the opposite sex who attempted to be my friend ended up dating me or one of my homeboys.

———

I didn't go to the office. I left school and headed over to Nick's. I had to tell him the truth.

"Yo, bro," I said to him. He was sitting on his building's steps, sprinkling weed and a sticky powder on top of a cigarillo. "I lost the gun."

"You what! A'yo what?!"

"It wasn't my fault. I was in the spot and—"

"Nigga, I'm joking," he laughed. "I mean, I'm mad at you, but bro, if you lost it, I know some wild shit happened."

He sealed the laced blunt with spit. I told him about the police raid.

"Fuck Homicide," he said. "I got two more guns tucked and you needa get your hands on one too. Issa war comin', niggas is dying this summer, be ready," he advised.

I wasn't thinking about beefing with nobody. I wasn't a shooter and didn't pretend to be one. Posers always get killed first. I was not desensitized to death, death still hurt—but I was used to the idea that something bad was going to happen. Someone would get shot—even if they were funny and cool and didn't deserve it like Don Don, someone would die. Dads would disappear—thankfully mine was now in rehab, but I knew I could lose him anytime. Uncles are found naked with hypodermic needles still deep in their flesh. And it might be you. If you are a man, you better take it. You better not cry or complain or say something stupid. You better not ask, "Why me?"

_____

She called around 11 p.m.

Her name was CC.

We talked, about everything. Her mom, her dad in jail for a double homicide, her block, my block, the politics of our high school, who was cool, who was a clown, who I should stay away from, her overdue papers, Nikes, new Nikes, more Nikes until she yelled, "Boy, I get it, you like Nikes! Shut the fuck up!" into the phone.

She was funny. I liked her. I really liked her, but not as a girlfriend. As an actual friend.

"Ya boyfriend go to our school?"

"Boy, please. My boyfriend is twenty-six," she laughed.

I thought about camp and how normal it must be for older people to take advantage of people like me, and how CC's boyfriend probably took care of her in ways that a kid my age couldn't. I just said, "If you ever need me, I'm around."

2

"You don't smoke no weed, right?" Dad laughed, driving up Harford Road. "Boy, you betta not be smoking no weed."

He knew I was high. He just didn't know how high I actually was. I was high, really high, high enough to shake God's hand. And I was happy too. I was happy because he was happy. Every question came with a smile and a giggle.

"Is you high?" Dad asked, sniffing and surveying me.

My eyes, hidden under my dark shades, were maroon after I domed three blunts with my friend Bernard. I knew Dad was coming to get me to run some errands, so I bathed myself in Polo Blue cologne. He knew I smoked weed, but I didn't want him to know that I smoked every day—all day. Mainly because he had been clean—no weed, no coke, no crack, not even booze. Dad had made a name for himself in Narcotics Anonymous—the magnetic personality that earned him praise in the streets and at the card games put the same spell on former users in the program, who'd phone him day and night in search of advice, an ear, or just a piece of his joy. Dad had it all in abundance. But my father didn't completely tackle the spirit of addiction—his new drug was food. Corned beef sandwiches smothered in mustard on rye, fried pepper steak with extra onions, sweet 7Up cakes, Ginger

Snaps cookies, sweet potato pies, fried fish, vanilla wafers, fried chicken, Big Macs, macaroni with eighty types of dairy, and steak subs, all washed down with Diet Coke.

"Nah,. Dad," I lied, giggling some more. "I ain't smoking no weed."

"Don't start with the weed, man, I'm tellin' you," Dad said. "One time I smoked too much weed and was driving up this street, right here, high as Fat Charles's ass!"

I laughed. "Who is Fat Charles?"

"Fat Charles had the highest ass in east Baltimore. He was six foot six, and his big ass sat right on the back of his neck!"

I couldn't stop laughing, I was too high for this. I was too high for anything. I was high as Fat Charles's ass. Giddy. My mouth was a desert, though, white foam caked up around my lips. I still couldn't stop laughing.

"I was so high," Dad continued, "that I side-swiped every car on this block, all thirty of them! Like boom, boom, boom…"

"And then what you do?" I laughed.

"What any responsible guy would do—I kept going!"

———

Weed and bullshit aside, I wanted to do something positive with my life—I wanted to be more than just another dope dealer. It wasn't a moral thing; I just looked in the mirror and saw a computer engineer or a lawyer staring back, not a criminal. But a little over a year after high school, like many people my age and from my block, I was sitting stiff at a two-chair kitchen table set, putting $3, $6, $10, $20, and $50 bags of blast together, with Nick.

Nick and I worked together. He had been hustling longer, but he talked too much and had a serious problem focusing. Plus he couldn't get the crack in the vial as quick as I could because his fingers were too fat. Nobody could cap as fast as me.

"We the next millionaires comin' out of Baldamore, D!" Nick would yell, flopping all over the place in our stash spot on Caroline Street. We were in the kitchen, surrounded by damaged drywall. Nick kept knocking dishes off the counter-top with his huge ass. "Look at all dis work!"

Growing up, I knew all the dealers, corner stragglers, nickel shavers, and block bosses. I even knew dudes who were juggling enough weight to sedate small towns. I had tried my hand before, made a few little transactions, but wasn't committed.

Nick and I had some quick success down on Curley Street with a product we branded as "Yeah Buddy." The cash poured in with steady traffic on a block that no one really paid attention to. Our little drug shop ran from about 4 p.m. to 8 p.m. It was an act of peace to split up times. The other guys who hustled on that block during the same shift were heroin dealers. We sold crack, so our clientele was completely different. The only other crack guys came out around 10 p.m. They were older dudes and many of them had day jobs. Everything was smooth until I heard some of them were calling their crack Yeah Buddy, pretending to be us.

"It's mainly that old nigga Clarence," Nick said, looking at his reflection in a chrome pistol. "If we handle him, the problem is solved."

I honestly didn't care if Clarence made a couple of dollars off of the Yeah Buddy name. He used to look out for me at the sneaker store when I was a kid and always played cards with my dad. *We can figure it out,* I thought. But my other father, the streets, couldn't tolerate it. If you let one person rip you off on Monday, you'd wake up to a million people lined up to get you on Tuesday.

I tucked my pistol in my hip and hopped shotgun in Nick's car. A wooden mini-slugger rested in the backseat. We drove down to Curley, just in time to see Clarence closing down his shop.

"Yo, Clarence!" I said. "You still selling Yeah Buddy?"

"Fresh out, young'un," he replied, shrugging his shoulders, spreading his arms. "What the fuck y'all want?"

I could hear Nick breathing, his body swelling.

"Ohhhhhhh shit!" Clarence yelled, tightening his eyes. He now recognized me. "Wassup, Lil Dwight! How ya fava doing? I ain't seen that nigga in years!"

I was going to tell Clarence that Dad was okay, and he couldn't use the name Yeah Buddy no more, and I was going to follow with a threat and some shit talk and maybe a joke or something. But then Nick swung the bat, cracking Clarence in the side of his head. And then another heavy CRACCC-CCCK! I stopped the third blow and kneeled down next to Clarence, blood flowing from his head.

"No more Yeah Buddy," I said. "I ain't asking."

Clarence got up holding his head. Nick cracked him again—and this time the bat broke, knocking him back to the ground. Nick pulled out his dick and aimed it at Clarence.

"Nah, bro," I said, pushing him away. "He get it."

"Don't get soft, D!" Nick replied, pissing in the gutter, away from Clarence, but close enough so that the splash from the stream could ricochet onto his limp body. "Don't get soft."

Beating Clarence boosted our reputations. Soon everyone was talking about how Nick and I cracked Clarence's head.

But that kind of reputation also had a downside. Working people in that neighborhood had known that Nick and I dibbled and dabbled, but we weren't looked at as violent drug dealers until that incident. We had traded the love we got from being goofy kids for fear, the kind that killers and cops that terrorized the neighborhood had. Nick saw it as a plus. I thought it was the dumbest thing we could've done.

"You cut out for this?" Nick asked.

"What?"

"I mean you talkin' to Clarence like you Dr. King or some shit. No talkin', you should've just bussed his head!"

Eventually, our hustle on Curley Street dried up. People started calling the cops on us. We'd get into little fights, some pointless beefs—the whole thing became a mess. We built a small crew and set up shop a few minutes away on Madeira Street.

There were no drug crews, competition, or heavy police activity when we built the shop on Madeira. The money started coming instantly, and fast too—so fast that we had to hire more help. But nothing is as easy as it seems.

———————

"Are you okay?" Dad asked on a phone call. "I ain't hear from you."

Hey! I'm on drugs and selling them too! I wanted to say. I wanted to tell him that I was making money, enough to pay his bills, enough to blow, and then some. I was my own man now. And that girls who wanted all of my money lovvvvvvvved me. Yet still, I felt like shit every day, and I drank every day, and sometimes I took pills, Oxys and Percs on top of the booze, until I felt fun and dizzy. I wanted to scream into the phone, *I'm an addict just like you used to be!*

"I'm good," I lied. "Maintaining, you know how it is."

"Yeah, man, I do," he laughed. "The more you cry…"

"The less you piss!" I finished.

It was hard to tell Dad what was going on with me. By now, I had the best house in our whole family, a house big enough for two families, two Mercedes, a CL 600 and CLK just to run errands in, and money busting out of my sweatpants pocket, my socks, the Nike boxes under my bed, my fireproof safe, and the closet in the stash house, and *still*, sometimes I wanted to die.

"You'll be fine," he said. "I love you son, talk soon." *Click*.

I was fucked up.

I wish he knew. And if he did know, then he probably heard that Nick and I were catching static from this dude named Dress-Code. He had just come home from the joint, Jessup Correctional Institution to be exact, and sent word to everyone hustling in the neighborhood that the block belonged to him, and we needed to. "Check in!" if we ever wanted to get any money around there.

A few days after Dress-Code's warning and after talking shit about each other to mutual friends, I spotted him. He was on the corner of Madeira and Ashland, leaning against a wall with one leg up, squeezing the neck of a Hennessy bottle. Dress-Code was surrounded by his crew, posing like a king on our throne. Nick and I were just coming back from an R&B concert in DC with a couple of girls. I told my date to pull the car over, reached in the glove box and pulled out my pistol, passed it to Nick, and jumped out of the car. "Dress, what's up man?" I said.

"I was lookin' for you, Lil D," he laughed as he approached

with a balled fist and landed a hard right across my jawline, so hard that I felt my teeth rattle. It dazed me. Nick got out of the car and sparked a blunt to watch the fight. I think he wanted to see if I was as invested as him, committed to dying for what we were trying to build. Dress-Code charged at me. I grabbed his shoulders and slung him to the ground. He popped me in the mouth and my lip burst. I swallowed the blood, still squared.

"D, whip his lil ass!" Nick yelled from the sidelines.

Dress-Code was little, but stronger than he looked.

We broke away from each other and started fresh. He charged at me again, I blocked him with my right hand and chopped his throat with my left. He backed off, grabbing his neck.

I pulled the gun out and slapped him across the face with it. I stood over him as he fell to the ground. Then I put both of my knees on his arms as I used the butt of the gun to beat some teeth out of his mouth. I beat him until his blood covered my shirt, until our blood mixed, until he was unconscious, until Nick pulled me off of him like, "Chill, D, you gonna kill him!"

In all fairness, I didn't have a problem with Dress-Code, but that didn't mean a thing. Beef isn't always who did what to who, not in our world—Nick and I found a spot that allowed us to make a lot of money, Dress-Code threatened that, so I had to beat on him until he rethought every decision he made leading up to him standing on that corner.

———

Nick and I were now running Madeira Street. You couldn't mention that block without our names coming up. We had real fans, groupies and wannabes.

We were making so much money that eventually the block became hotter than fish grease. One day, a cop ran up on me while I was just sitting on the steps, drinking a bottle of water, and slammed me up against a wall. Then he slammed me into his car. "I know exactly who you are, Lil Dwight!" he said. "I see what you got going on around here!" I didn't know who he was. Eventually I'd learn that he was Mike Fries. Stupid name.

"I don't know you, man, wrong guy," I said, turning my face away as he dug into my pockets. He took some of my cash and told me to be on my way.

"Nick, we gotta get off this block, it's too hot," I warned.

"You worry too much, D, we good."

We weren't good.

BOOK IV

a first love story

20–21 years old, 2000–2001

"I won't ever leave you, even though
you're always leaving me."
—Audrey Niffenegger

1

"Yo, Watkins, you a dog, yo. You don't know how to treat women!" Tweety Bird said, a big smile covering her face.

I spit some barbecue sunflower seeds into a brown paper bag. "Yeah, if I was a girl I definitely wouldn't date me." Tweety Bird had a big head and big mouth attached to a small body. Her heart was bigger than the whole of east Baltimore, and she smiled as much as she blinked.

Tweety was Troy's main girlfriend and basically his heart. "Tweety my heart," he'd sob, sometimes for no reason at all. "Tweety Bird my heart, yo. She's my everything!" I thought it was pathetic, but he'd come a long way since letting Burger spit shrimp shells on his face, and Tweety was a great woman.

Tweety was loving and always kind. I'd tease her by calling her a "light-skinned lollipop" any chance I'd get. She hated it and would shoot both of her middle fingers at me, but in the next minute go on and on saying "I love you so so much, bro." And to quell the mushiness I'd do something nasty like lick my finger and stick it into her food. "You still love me?"

Hanging with Troy, and therefore Tweety, was everything. Troy had a gift for fixing and figuring out computers, and he was my only close friend who didn't sell drugs—the rest of us were outlaws, always hustling, always strapped, and always caught up in something. Troy and I didn't talk drugs all day long—I liked that he had a girl, goals, ambitions, and stories that stretched beyond the crumbled pavement of our block. Troy was in college. He had once gone whitewater rafting. He did things I never thought of, like applying to jobs in Miami and Toronto. "Bro, I'm flying to Toronto to see about this job," he'd say on a corner full of us dope dealers. We weren't going anywhere and we knew it. Some dudes would hate, like, "Yo, Troy, you really think you gonna be something, nigga, you ain't shit!"

I still always had Troy's back, that was my duty. "Man, shut the fuck up and listen! Troy, please finish."

I wanted to hear more about what life in a place like Toronto or Miami would be like. I hung on Troy's every word.

Me: Would the streets be the same in Canada?
Troy: Hell no.
Me: Could I learn to surf in Miami and cut up on the waves every day?
Troy: Hell yeah.

Troy's skills on the computer had grown far beyond what we could have imagined back when we were nine and toying with Game Boys. He could code before anybody knew what coding was. He was the first one around the way to own a desktop. He could also fix anything, from brake pads and cracked transmissions to kitchen cabinets. Troy worked at a clinic not too far from the block we hustled on. He'd come home after he got off to hang with us, still wearing his uniform, a set of loose blue scrubs, with creases in the sleeves and pants, his ID badge, beat Air Max, and a plastic G-Shock watch.

Troy's favorite lines and motto used to be, "Selling drugs is gonna land you in jail, D. Let's start a legal business, like a store or car dealership."

I never took business advice from Troy because he got looped into countless pyramid schemes like Amway and Quixtar, and he lived off of overtime.

And then Troy changed. The more the rest of us grew in the streets, the more he became hypnotized by our jewelry and the clothes we'd wear from designers like Gucci and Louis Vuitton. We'd play full-court basketball in new Prada sneakers, and often gave them away when the games ended. He was obsessed with the cars we drove—I had a 600 Benz, a Lexus SC430, Nick had a Range Rover and S 500, and we had a few Cadillac Escalades in the crew. We never talked about car payments. We didn't know anything about that. Troy would compare the thousands of dollars I flaunted and blew to what he earned at work after clocking in for ninety-plus hours. Troy had a boss that constantly breathed down his neck for petty shit. I was my own boss. However, I honestly didn't want Troy in the game and would have paid him to stay away, but one day he popped up with his own connect, so I had to school him.

Troy walked in on me counting up, once. "Got damn, bro!" he yelled. "That gotta be a hundred thousand dollars!" Troy never saw that much money in his life. His eyes bulged. It was really more like $20,000, but it looked like a fortune to him, a year's salary. "Can I touch it?" he asked. I tossed a few stacks in his direction. It was street money, all tattered 10s, 5s, and 1s, not crisp bank bills. Street money is fluffy, faded, written on, and every dollar had a story. Small stories piled up into books, libraries, and my freedom. I called money "Freedom paper." Troy wanted to taste that freedom, and since he had a connect, he was in. He begged me to be part of it until I couldn't tell him no anymore. And working with Troy meant working with his pint-sized love, his heart, Tweety.

Tweety was originally from North Carolina, but didn't have an accent—or at least not what a Baltimorean thought a Carolinian should sound like. For hours, we'd post up in my trap house, me cooking product or giving money to runners, Tweety packaging work, and Troy doing a little bit of all while we'd debate about various topics. Today we were discussing my chaotic dating life and having a humorous discussion over which were better—the Jordan 4s or 5s. Troy and I agreed that the 3s were the best. "I'll give you that, Watkins," Tweety squeaked, digging deep into her large Gucci bag, pulling out a half-smoked blunt. "You wouldn't date you, at least you know yourself."

"I'm not smoking that," I said, walking over to crack the window—it was tricky, you had to jiggle it out of position and tilt, to pull it up or down. We were at my hangout spot, the place where I held meetings with the crew, where we played video games into the wee hours, and where I took girls who I didn't want to bring to my real place. It was a tiny two-bedroom, directly across from our stash house.

Tweety placed the blunt between her lips, pulled out a 99-cent gas station lighter, and flicked a few flames out, before throwing it onto the floor. "This broke-ass shit!"

"Yo, I told you stop buying those cheap lighters, they only last three days, get a Bic," I said, holding my lighter up under her frazzled blunt and letting the flame burn as she took a long pull. She blew out a cloud of gray smoke away from the recliner where I slouched observing her.

"So, who you spendin' your birthday with?" she asked.

"Sharon, Nay Nay, Shannon, La Tesha, Shanekia, the girl Tinka, Peaches, Peaches's cousin?"

"I don't know, maybe all of them," I laughed, pondering. "Maybe none. I didn't put much thought into it, it's just a birthday."

"Nigga what?" she coughed, hacking, her tiny eyes watering until she caught her breath. "Yo, your birthday in like three days, that's big shit! You know those girls got plans. You gotta grow up, boy."

"I'm single."

"These girls are fighting to make you happy. Shannon saved up to buy you them $200 Pippens!"

With all due respect, Shannon was one of the coolest girls that I was dating. She loved basketball, and could name every blue-chip player in college, and never really bothered me like everyone else for liking shows like HBO's *Curb Your Enthusiasm*. She'd watch it with me, and acquired her own taste for satire. However, she had a boyfriend. He was locked up, and she'd always swear they weren't together, but did he know that? I also knew she'd be at that jail visiting him every week.

"Oh yeah? What color did she get?" I asked, looking at the stacks of sneaker boxes that lined the wall. Boxes on boxes in rows that touched the floor and ceiling.

"Do it matter what color? Nigga, these girls broke, that's what I'm sayin'. You gotta think, Watkins, everybody don't do what we do for money."

"Look, she asked me what I wanted, mind you, and I told her nothing. You gotta realize I never asked her to buy me anything, I can get my own Pippens."

Tweety rolled her eyes. "Watkins, you ever tell them that there's other girls competing for your affection? Yo, for you to be so smart, you really dumb." She took another pull. I watched her exhaling the smoke and then pulling it back into her lips.

Tweety was probably right. She had become Troy's main girl. It was hard for me and most of my homies to commit, but Troy did. He'd cheat on her and get caught, they'd break up and get back together, and then she'd cheat on him, and they'd break up again and get back together.

"Never thought about it like that," I said, digging into my pocket and pulling out my own weed, a fat fuzzy nugget with hints of blue, stored inside a tightly sealed glass jar. The whole neighborhood was smoking blueberry at the time—exotic strands were new to us. They were beautiful-looking and hit way harder than the mid dirt weed called Arizona we were used to. I took a loose cigarillo and removed it from the plastic, split it with my ring finger, dumped the innards into a bag of chewed-up sunflower seed shells, dabbed the paper with a little spit, pieced off morsels from the blue fuzzy nugget, loaded the paper, and sealed it with my torch. I laid back with the lit blunt and took a long pull, filling my lungs and the room with a thick cloud of smoke that dampened and reddened my eyes. I didn't need a girl, I had fancy marijuana. Weed was 30 percent of my diet. I probably puffed an ounce every two to three days.

"I take that back," I said, eyeing Tweety through the dissipating cloud of smoke that just floated out of my lungs. "I would definitely date a nigga like me."

"Oh yeah?"

"I'm young and I can pay for everything. Everything. I pay when I take these girls out. I buy them earrings, clothes, and get their braids done or their perms or tracks or sew-ins or whatever the fuck they want. Shit, I bought Shay Shay's mother a couch, they were sitting on the floor. I bought Ronnie a bed to get her off that air mattress she had to blow up every night. I do what I say I'm gonna do, always. I always wear rubbers; I ain't got no kids or crazy baby muvas. I don't beat them up, not even if they hit me first. And I don't care if any of them fuck around with another dude cuz it ain't my business."

Tweety grabbed her head like it ached. "You men always want credit for stuff y'all supposed to do! Dummy, you not supposed to hit girls, you supposed to pay for dinner and get her hair done, that's real nigga shit, mandatory," she said, laughing.

"Gimme my credit, Tweety!" I laughed, even though she was starting to make me upset. I know I did everything these women asked me to do. "Gimme my credit, Tweety!" I repeated, beating my chest.

"Seriously, though, Watkins, who are you committed to, my nigga?"

"Me!" I said. "Besides, where would these girls be if I was broke? You saying Shannon spending $200 on some shoes I didn't ask for, some shoes I probably already got. Ask me how much I spent on her?!"

"Nigga, is everything a transaction?"

"Yeah!"

"You crazy," Tweety said, shaking her big round head. "I'm just saying, stop being so nice if you aren't going to let them return the favor, that crushes women. And you are killing them."

2

"I hate Tweety! That fuckin' bitch!" Troy yelled at 3 a.m. a week prior, after I fell asleep at their crib. He hollered so loud when he saw her at the door that he probably woke the entire block up. "Don't let her in here ever again!"

They were having one of their infamous fights, and unfortunately, I was once again stuck in the middle of it. A week ago, it was "I fuckin' love Tweety, she a queen, bro."

"Word," I replied, as I forced broken pieces of crack into small vials.

"I need her, bro, she a real fuckin' Black yellow-skinned queen," he pleaded for me to understand like his life depended on it.

"Put a ring on it, then, nigga," I always replied. My response had become automatic after dealing with their dysfunction. I never knew what to expect. Keeping up with them made me dizzy.

Every day, every level of their relationship was intense. Like the time she had her period and he kept calling her hormones "whore-moans." It pissed her off so bad that she tried to run him over with his car. The time he *thought* she was cheating on him so he beat her cousin's ass for not telling him, when actually he was the one cheating with the drunk lotto lady from across the alley. The time she flung a pot of steaming hot grits at him in a rage—almost hitting me! The times they'd wake me up at 4 a.m. to share an inside joke between them that I could never get. The time we strapped up with guns and combed the city for two days straight because she was missing. The time they beat the shit out of our corner man for a reason only God knows. The time she cracked me in the head with a Timberland boot as I choked Troy during a heated argument. The time I found them passed out on Ashland Avenue during a blizzard after they'd been making snow angels, and I threw my back out dragging their drunk bodies home. The many drunk nights where all three of us vowed to never drink again, and ended up more drunk the next day. The many times they took the last slice of pizza from me and split it with each other. When they bailed each other out of jail. The time when we all bought Jordan 3s and they fought because Troy left the bags on top of the car. All of the pregnancy scares and the *I love yous* and the *I hate yous* and everything in between. They worked my nerves, but somehow I wanted a love like they had. I wanted somebody who I was willing to go crazy over, somebody that was willing to go crazy over me, somebody I needed. I didn't think I needed anybody.

A week later it was Tweety: "His Black ass fuckin' around with another bitch!" she yelled repeatedly to me into the phone as I watched Troy sneak KeKe from Jefferson Street out the back door. "Where he at, Watkins?!"

The next day it was "That is my Black-ass baby, I love him so much, Watkins. You just don't know how much I love his chocolate ass!"

And she was right. I didn't.

3

"Yo, we out, bro," Troy said, flopping on the couch Tweety had dozed off on, so hard that it moved and woke her up. She adjusted her head on his lap and tried to resume her nap.

I checked the stash and Troy was right, all of the product was gone. Our work for the day was done. Tweety unfurled from Troy's lap, stretching her arms and legs and cracking her bones. "Yo, happy birthday, Watkins, you fuckin' old-ass nigga!"

"Oh, shit, bro!" Troy yelled. "Why you ain't tell me?! I ain't know!"

I shrugged. "It's February tenth every year, it actually never changes."

The duo hit me with a barrage of plans—drinking, smoking, snorting ("Hell no, I don't snort!"), girls, a party, more girls, a strip club, all of the strip clubs, a seafood platter, shrimps, lobster, crab cakes, a road trip, a cruise, they pleaded.

"We gotta work, we aren't regular twenty-year-olds Troy, there's no road trip, and blackout days for us," I said. "You know how hard it was to get this block, this clientele, and to keep it?"

I wasn't being ungrateful, but we had a dope shop to run. The fiends need their product, and it's our job to get it to them or risk losing our corners to somebody else who could. Times like this I knew Troy wasn't cut out for this life. He should've moved to Miami if he wanted a cruise and to do road trips.

"Aight, I'm gonna get some drinks and some pizzas," Troy said, sensing my frustration, "and chicken too."

"Nigga, it's breakfast time, 11 a.m.!" Tweety interrupted. "Fuck some pizza, let's cook a brunch! Buy brunch ingredients! Brunch! Brunch! Brunch!"

"What the fuck is brunch?" Troy asked.

"It's between breakfast and lunch," I said, "but I wanna eat pizza. It's my birthday, fuck a brunch."

"Pizza it is!" Troy said, walking out of the door.

"I was gonna cook you an eight-star meal, fool, and you want some stankin' pizza," Tweety said, sprinkling a small pinch of cocaine on the tip of her tiny index finger.

"I don't like home-cooked meals."

"What kinda nigga don't like home-cooked meals?" She snorted, then paused to frantically pat her nose like it was on fire. "You really don't like cooked meals?"

I thought about Dad's fried crab cakes. He'd make them tiny and round, and as soon as he took them out of the frying pan, he'd dab the grease off and watch me eat them, impatiently waiting for me to tell him how good they were. His other specialty was pan-seared pepper steak made in his favorite faded, bent cast-iron pan. He'd flood the steak with a bunch of seasoning, carefully sliced onions, and green peppers, and serve it over hot Uncle Ben's rice. He'd make spaghetti, but I hated spaghetti as much as I hated liver, meatloaf, and drippy eggs.

My mother wasn't the best cook. She was a young mom, and had to spend more time caring for us than my dad, while figuring out the world around her. But she could probably win a trophy for her scrambled eggs. They were always fluffy, bright yellow, and not too buttery, perfection. Now, Mom's chicken was dryer than sandpaper, her Rice-A-Roni that stuck to the pan was even dryer. She'd serve it with dry canned vegetables; she even figured out a way to make dry soup. I explained to Tweety that I pay for food.

Famma, my beautiful grandma, was a great cook, but there were like forty children, grandchildren, and great-grandchildren running in and out of her house. So, after many of our big family dinners, I still ended up eating McDonald's or 60-cent rice and gravy from the Korean corner store with the clouded bulletproof glass window. My older cousins' fat bellies would fall over their waistlines as they bragged about how good the stuffin' was. When I got older, I made it a point to feed my nephews and little cousins first.

Dad loved cooking food, sharing it, and talking about it. I loved paying for it.

"The way to a man's heart is through his stomach," Tweety said. "My Big Momma was never single cuz she could burn."

"I don't care about that, Tweety," I said. "I would proudly cheat on your grandma right after eating my favorite dish!"

We laughed.

Women always threw out cooking for me as a way to pull me in, but I had money to eat gourmet cuisines at nice places. What Tweety and other women didn't seem to understand was that the last way to my heart was through feeding me. At this point I built my life around always doing whatever I wanted to do. I knew what I needed, and it wasn't a woman like Tweety to dictate, or a home-cooked plate—just money, freedom, and constant work.

———

Troy burst through the door with two large hot pizzas and a family-sized chicken box stacked in one hand, and the biggest bottle of Belvedere I had ever seen in the other. I jumped up, grabbed some paper plates, and snatched two slices before they could dig in.

"Troyyyy baby," Tweety said. "Why this fool only eat takeout?"

"What's wrong with only eating takeout?" Troy answered, shoving a whole slice into his mouth. "Ain't no dishes with takeout."

We laughed and I poured myself a big birthday cup of vodka, splashing it with Arizona Iced Tea, just enough to change the color from clear to light-light brown, and took a big burning swig.

"Did Shannon get ya shoes?" Tweety asked, pulling some of the excess cheese off her slice.

"I guess," I replied. "I don't want them."

"Huh? Why you doing her like that, Watkins?"

"I'll take them!" Troy said.

"Yo, I don't want nobody stressing over me."

"No food, no gifts? Damn, you cold, nigga," Tweety said. "Who in the fuck hurt you?"

Who hurt me? It could've been the girl Nell or Toya from eighth grade, or Shay, she was my soul mate back in the seventh until she developed curves, outgrew me, and was gone, just like Nikki from sixth grade who left me for a tenth grader that had a mustache. Could've been Nay or Takia, my fifth-grade crush. There was the lady at camp who I still thought about from time to time—the image of her face still made me cringe and pull my lashes out. I don't know, but by high school, I was burned out—not really interested in romance, dates, love, or anything loving. Sappy wasn't cool— dudes who bought heart-shaped balloons to school for their girls' birthdays or Valentine's Day could be seen crying in the cafeteria after finding out their love was spotted climbing out of my car.

I'd freely tell every girl I gave my number to that we were a couple and then laugh when my girlfriends met and sometimes fought after finding out they weren't the only one. None of this, the rage or wind of emotions, bothered me.

"That nigga ain't hurt," Troy huffed, inhaling chicken wings, spitting out the bones. "He a hoe."

I laughed. Tweety looked at Troy. "Watkins just nice enough to not have a girlfriend."

"That nigga ain't nice!" Troy chuckled. "He always been cold!"

Troy stood up, knocking boxes off of the table, locking eyes with me, slurred speech spitting. "Yo, D used to kick girls out of his house by cranking up the AC in the winter, sayin' that the heat is broke!"

I shrugged. "Sometimes you wanna be alone after you finish. All Black girls from Baltimore are anemic, so the cold works."

"Asshole!" Tweety yelled.

"Oh, I got a thousand stories," Troy continued.

"Nah, I'm not that cold!" At least, I thought I wasn't. No one had ever confronted me on the way I treated women, except Tweety. *Who hurt me?* Maybe it was my first heart break, literally a broken heart.

Back when I was in the second grade, my teacher, a frumpy white lady with a wide country face, had us roll a dough-like substance into wide flat rectangle sheets. She then gave us heart-shaped cookie cutters and said, "Cut out as many as you want, we are going to bake them until they are as hard as cement and paint them for Mother's Day!"

My Mother's Day gifts normally consisted of a card that my dad purchased and wrote my name in, or some monstrosity that I constructed in art class with glue, construction paper, and tape. However, this was nice, this would be art. This was going to be a handmade, custom-painted piece of art with my mom's name carved into it, by me. I had cut out three hearts just in case I messed up, but I got it right on the first try.

"Wow, Mr. Watkins," my art teacher said. "Your mother is going to love this! Please show the class." I stood up and slowly waved my perfectly shaped pink heart with a red center— *I love you* on one side, Mom's name on the other. On the way home from school, I bought pink wrapping paper with a pink card and a matching pink gift bag. It was an impressive presentation for a seven-year-old. Once I reached the house, I sat it up on the table, all trophy-like, a proud display of my labor and celebration of my mom, the woman I loved most in the world.

Mom came home from work drained, cranky.

"Look, Ma!" I said, wide-eyed and proud. "Open it!"

"I had a long day," she yawned. "I'll open it later, let me get some rest."

It was fine, I figured she'd open it on Sunday, Mother's Day. Then Sunday came, and another and another. Her gift just sat on the table, untouched, still in the bag. She didn't even look at it. Maybe Mom was stressed with school or work, or Dad's addiction, or raising three kids in the most violent city in America, I don't know. I didn't know about any of that. I was just pissed that the gift I worked so hard on wasn't even acknowledged.

About two weeks later, I dug into the bag, pulled the heart out, and threw it against the wall, watching it explode into little pieces. *Fuck this shit*, I thought. I grabbed a broom, swept up my broken heart, and threw it in the trash can.

"Hey Ma," I said to her a few days later, when she came in after work. "Did you like the heart I made? Where is it at?"

"Oh yeah, I liked it a lot," she said. "It's on my desk at work."

4

"One day, I'm gonna have a lady and I'm gonna treat her right," I told Tweety as I poured another glass of vodka and lit a new blunt.

"If you say so, Watkins," Tweety laughed. "Maybe you damaged goods."

"Okay, okay, her name was Shardé," I said. "She was my first love, yo, back when I was twelve and Shardé was much older."

"That big-forehead light-skinned singer?" Tweety said, smirking.

"Sweet taboo is my shit, bruh!" Troy yelled, now drunk and slumped. "Sweetest tabooooooooooo! Ohhhh, ohhhhh."

"Yo, nigga, that's Sade," I said, "This girl name was S-H-A-R-D-E."

"Oh. Burger's freak-ass cousin?" Troy asked, confused.

"Chill, yo, she wasn't a freak," I laughed.

"Man, fuck Burger, I hated that nigga when we was little," Troy said, taking a swig. "His cousin was fine, though."

Shardé was twenty-two years old, track star lean, with sleek cat-like features. She was Burger's older cousin, but you would never think that lumpy troll was related to an angel like her. I'd go to their apartment, 1B, to see Burger, *really*

Shardé, and sit in the living room for hours, stuck to their pleather couch playing NBA Live while she'd prance around in satin waist-length negligées. My favorite was the powder blue two-piece. Unlike most twelve-year-olds, I wasn't crazy about video games. I just wanted to catch a glimpse of Shardé and to do grown things with her. She'd *Black Swan* through the living room half-naked and my chest would freeze. Every time she passed the living room, it felt like my heart took a trip up a roller coaster. I'd eye her and blush when she noticed. I'm too dark to blush, but I know she noticed, and Burger would slap me out of it in disgust.

"Move on outta here," he'd tell her. "Nobody want your raggedy ass!" She'd wink, spark a Newport, and whip her silky curls away from her face before capering back into her room. Shardé was a clean almond color all over—she never had a blemish—just a smile and the longest legs I'd ever seen under a set of hips that spread. On days I got new haircuts, she'd always notice, and made a point to stand over me wide-legged, examining my fade, claiming that I was going to drive all of the little girls "bat-shit crazy." Shardé was the best part of my day and didn't even know it.

"Why you act all goofy and shit when she come by, like you never saw a fuckin' hoe before!" Burger said one day. I waved him off like, "Shut up, man, she ain't no hoe, cut the game on!"

"D, you must don't know what a hoe is!" he laughed. "She is literally a hoe in every sense of the word."

I could have played NBA Live at home or gone over to anyone else's house, but Shardé wasn't anywhere but there. Burger didn't have many friends, we all just kind of outgrew his bullshit. Shardé moving in with him was the only reason I tolerated him and played at their house. He'd told me that Shardé was a "hooker," what we now call sex workers, and he would collect money from the "johns," or her *clients*, making him like a business partner or enforcer. He'd grown from an oversized child to an oversized teenager who could easily be mistaken for a man. Burger would post up in the living room, small gun poking through the waistline of his jeans—the handle showing from under his dingy Hanes T-shirt. From there, he'd watch as customers migrated in and out. I noticed that most of them came in anxious or nervous-looking, but they all left relaxed. Gold roped-up street dudes, broke orange-reflector-vested city workers, Jheri-curled Baptist reverends, and thirsty-ass collared up married men who would gladly spend all of their kids' Christmas money just to get a whiff of her—all would slide through at different times of the day. The operation ran like clockwork: pay Burger $200 for the hour, bust a nut in fifteen minutes or less, and then leave, giving her time to clean herself up in between clients.

"You ever shot somebody?" I asked Burger, eyeing the pistol on his side.

"Yeah, lil nigga, and one day, you will too," he said, peeling that gun off of his waist and placing it into my hands. "That's just how it goes. Them or you."

I fondled the pistol, touching every piece of it, the rusty barrel, the muzzle, the grooves on the revolver, the trigger, the hammer, the front sight, the nicked wooden handle. And I opened it, touched the cylinders, rubbed the ratchet, and closed it. I looked at it, absorbed the power, what it could do to me, or to another person.

I turned around and aimed it at the door and then at Burger. I could shoot him in the same spot. *I'll murder ya fat ass*, I thought. I noticed the dent where I had knocked the chunk of meat out of his head so many years ago.

"Nigga, don't point that shit at me! Unless you ready to use it!" Burger breathed, frantically slapping the pistol away from me and placing it in his lap. He reached over and put me in a tight-ass headlock, my forehead and mouth smothered by his fat underarm meat. He squeezed until I almost passed out, before letting me go. Burger picked up the joystick. "You pull a gun on a nigga, you better use it. And I don't care who on the other end because if you let them go, they gonna get you. One of these thirsty horny niggas hurt Shardé or try to steal, I'm killin' them!"

"What you gonna do with the body?"

"I'll pack their thirsty ass up and dump them at this lil spot by south Baldamore, but don't ask questions about where bodies go. You don't need to know the answer to shit like that unless you ready to kill," Burger said, shooting me an ice-cold stare. "Huh? You ready to kill a nigga?"

"You ever hide a body before?"

Burger looked at me and turned away. I imagined what he'd do to me if he ever knew how thirsty I was for Shardé. Maybe he knew. Her clients wanted to kill themselves when she was booked, had taken a day off, or was on her period. Sometimes she'd make fun of the dudes who brought her Motrins, chocolates, tampons, and paid for "platonic time only" during her menstrual cycle. "Sometimes I let them fuck me while I'm bleeding, they freak niggas like that," she once told us. "I just lay a towel down and throw it away afterwards." Shardé called all of her clients clowns. She would always tell us that she'll never get married, because 99 percent of breathing men ain't shit, and the other 1 percent are taken.

"I'ma be a good man," I told her as she walked in my direction one afternoon. "Watch, I'ma treat my lady right."

"Yeah, cuz you a baby, wait till you start fuckin'," she

said slow into my ear, her lips brushing across the side of my face.

"Nobody would ever marry ya dirty ass anyway," Burger said. "Nobody in they right mind would marry a hoe!"

She frowned her nose. *I'd marry her*, I thought. I couldn't say it, but I thought it. Burger would always attack her looks, her profession, their life—a life that paid their rent, paid for their food and the clothes on his back. I felt like he was jealous of her beauty, the money she made, and the amount of people that craved her attention. Shardé was a desire magnet and everybody knew, even Burger.

"Only thing you gonna marry is ya right hand with ya fat ass!" Shardé would clap back. "Probably won't never feel the inside of a pussy. Keep all ya little porn tapes, you gonna need it."

Burger once showed me his porn stash. He kept it in a brown cardboard box that was busted around the edges. Inside was a collection of titles like *Black Ebony Orgy*, *Black Bubble Booty*, *Bad Black Hoes*, etc. He said I could borrow them, but I declined. I wasn't really into porn, and his tapes were probably covered in dried-up fluids.

My pre-Shardé wardrobe was all basketball clothes—a jersey of whatever team I balled for, matching shorts, and whichever of my Air Jordans matched or didn't. But after I laid eyes on Shardé, you couldn't catch me in nothing but a new Polo, Nautica, or Hilfiger shirt, with matching sweats or designer jeans. Shardé would compliment me on everything I wore, it felt like she noticed it all. "Oh baby, that shirt cute!"

"Oh, you can have it," I'd say smugly, as if it was nothing, as if I wasn't draining every resource I had to get my twelve-year-old hands on those clothes.

Shardé knew I liked her. She flirted, playing with me, calling me sweetie and her lil fiancé. I knew she only saw me as a little boy, Burger's friend, or would always see me as a kid until I did something about it, so I decided to step to her. I wanted to show her that I was a man. One day, I hit up the apartment when I knew Burger wasn't home. Shardé opened the door half-naked as usual—a black nightie slipping off of her shoulder. "Burger not here, cutie, but you can come in."

I walked in and sat on the corner of the couch. I'd never been alone with her before. Burger's porn collection stared back at me. My heart pounded, every beat vibrated through my body. I kept checking my fit—my Jordan 7s looked good, my clothes were new and flawless.

"Wanna smoke, babe?" she said from the other room.

"Yeah, I got some fire!" I replied, making my voice deeper than what it was.

She came and sat close enough for me to touch her, but I didn't. She sliced the blunt with her narrow finger—its cocoa-colored insides snowed onto the stained carpet. Surrounding us was spilled food, empty cold cups, Hennessy bottles, more blunt guts, and old Chinese food containers, all Burger's, he never put his trash in the can. I passed her a fluffy light green bud. She sniffed it. "This is some good-ass shit, baby boy! Where you be getting this?"

"Oh, it's more where that came from."

Shardé sat on the couch with her legs folded like a pretzel. She stuffed the nugget into a small metal box and started grinding the bud into crushed-parsley-sized flakes. She then packed the blunt, rolled it tight, and sealed it with two wet kisses.

"How you learn how to roll so quick?"

"Time is precious, baby, don't waste any, never ever," she said. "Time is the main factor in everything I do."

She sparked the joint, and after two puffs each, we were both sitting on clouds. I couldn't stop staring at her. I could do this all day, for the rest of my life. She noticed me looking and wrapped her arms around my shoulders, and blew a bubble of smoke into my face, capped with a light giggle. "You gonna be driving the ladies crazy when you get older, boy. I know it. You gotta little girlfriend?" she asked, pulling back. I wanted to grab her, pull her back close to me, but I maintained my cool.

"Naw, just me."

"I don't believe you, you gotta girl," she said, taking another puff. "And why you always skippin' school?"

"I don't know," I said, reaching for the blunt, taking a pull.

"I bet you end up with one of those high yellow college girls, like the ones on A *Different World*, ha!" She took the blunt from me, ashed it, puffed, ashed it again, and then passed it back to me. "Schoolboy, you should be in school?"

"That's my favorite show. Dwayne Wayne got all the Jordans. But why you sayin' I'm a schoolboy, tho?"

"Because you ain't like Burger's dumb ass, that nigga can't even tell time on a digital clock. You special. You ain't gonna be stuck around here forever like him, or me."

"You ain't gotta be stuck here."

"What, you gonna take me up outta this? You gonna save me from the projects, cutie?" she giggled, surveyed the room, and then focused her eyes on me. "I remember when I was a baby like you. I had so many dreams. I wanted to be a doctor or chef, but I can't even cook toast."

"It's easy, just drop the bread in and press down on the lever."

I laughed. She laughed too. We were quiet for a while. I rolled another blunt. We smoked, giggled some more, and smoked again.

"You should be leaving soon. Burger ain't gonna be back for a while and you ain't fillin' in for him," she said. I wanted to stay forever, or at least long enough to state my feelings, but she had clients coming by. Money had to be made. She offered me $30 for the weed we split, as if I was a child. And even though I was a child, I rejected it.

"Don't let ya life go by without doing anything, baby," she said. "Be something, stop hanging around here so much, we ain't got shit goin' on."

"What you mean?"

"I mean school, college. Be a plumber, they make good money," she said, taking one big pull from the blunt and pulling me close to blow smoke into my face. "Don't do what these boys do 'round here, cutie. Do more. Be a real somebody."

"Okay, I will."

"And when you make it, don't be forgettin' about me, baby."

The smoke followed me out of her unit. There was no dramatic ending. I just stopped hanging around their apartment. Burger would go in and out of jail over the next few years, for armed robbery, breaking and entering, and various assault charges. After his last prison stretch, Burger had built up a crew and was hustling on a corner that belonged to some older guys from the neighborhood. They started a mini war but eventually squashed it, agreeing to occupy the corner at different times, so they said. Then someone put out a rumor about him being a snitch. It was basically a death sentence. The snitching allegation couldn't be solved with fists. Burger was shot in the back seventeen times after leaving a corner store near the block where he hustled. Rumor had it that the shooter pissed on him as the smoke drifted out of the holes in his corpse. The dudes he fought swore they had nothing to do with it, and maybe they didn't, but my crew and I never asked any questions because, again, he wasn't a part of us.

Shardé was covered in grief at his funeral. Her soft baby face had aged thirty years in under a decade, I imagine from all of the smoking, drinking, and fast food. She gave me a big hug at the repast and I pulled back to look at the bruises on her face, her missing front teeth. "You taking care of yourself?" I asked.

"I'm doing okay, but not as good as you, schoolboy," she said, looking me up and down. "I gotta lil job at the MCI call center, but off weekends, come see me sometime."

Troy and Tweety looked at me as I told my story, then paused, and then both burst into gut-busting laughter. Their laughter exploded in multiple directions—every tooth in Troy's mouth exposed, Tweety's face turning from yellow to a shade of red, as I sat there, vulnerable, looking like a square. "This is why I don't tell y'all clowns anything!" I said, downing my vodka, refilling the cup, downing that too.

"Hol' up, hol' up," Troy laughed, falling to his knees, pounding the floor like a drum. "You were twelve and you didn't know how to buy pussy from a MCI call center hooker? It's easy, it only cost $40," he hollered.

"No, that's a lady," Tweety hissed, "if she would've touched him, it would've been rape."

"Men can't get raped, Tweety!" Troy breathed. "Shut ya dumb ass up!"

"Both of y'all need to shut up!" I yelled.

They had a nerve to talk, I thought. The amount of drama between them made me nauseous. I could have any girl I wanted. Their love thing was all crying, heartache, and pain. Shardé didn't do anything negative to me—as a matter of fact, she protected me by telling me to stay away from that apartment—but she had the power to suck me up into that kind of trance where I'd be blinded and dumb like them, and that wasn't happening. I'd do anything to avoid somebody having that kind of power over me.

"You'll never be happy!" Tweety belted out.

"What I do is safe!"

"I'll drink to that!" Troy echoed.

"Money is safe, distance is safe!" I shouted. The both of them, as drunk as me, barking franticly like rabid dogs, so loud it was disturbing—but not really, because this was how we acted.

"Safe? We sell narcotics!" Tweety clapped back.

"You know what I mean?" Troy nodded in agreement.

"The past is the past, Watkins!" Tweety argued. "Living in the past shits on your future, don't you ever forget that."

I was taught to chase money. Dad drilled in me, "Always, always get ya money! Fuck everything else!" The girls said the men who couldn't pay for dinner were jokes, to be laughed at—unworthy of coming around. ("Why is this nigga even talkin', he broke!") This was the rule, spoken or unspoken. It didn't matter if a dude was smart, funny, handsome, had potential, or all of the above—because those things cannot feed people. If you are a man, you better have money. Shardé only spent time around men with money. She had no boyfriend or love interest.

"Aye Shardé, you ever go on dates? Like to big-money

restaurants where a guy in a black vest plays the violin while you eat?"

"What? Hell no. You gonna take me?"

And I would've taken her in a minute—and I would've encouraged her to eat and drink all she wanted, and then we could've hit a movie, or the club, or both, and all of that cost money.

Tweety was a homie and Troy's love, but their union was far from cheap. Their relationship was the strongest when we ate good, big crab cakes stuffed with shrimp, top-shelf liquor, and all the extras—when we were driving Benzes and BMWs, chasing each other like kids on city bikes, running red lights and stop signs, tapping each other's bumpers; when we kept her paid, and on vacation in Jamaica or the Dominican Republic or Cancún dressed in new designer everything, Gucci, Louis, and Dior. But when the money dried up, and Troy left the drug game, her connection to him broke apart like a cheap wineglass—the both of them shattering in multiple directions, no more loud fighting or crazy arguments, no "I love you"s. She cheated out in the open, almost daring him to find out, as if "Why is this nigga even talkin', he broke!"

Tweety found a new man. He was in a crew of wild gunslingers who were the new money-getters from a neighborhood that was close to ours. We knew them all, but we never hated. Tweety would come around every once in a while to visit, still fly, still stick skinny. She still loved us and just wanted to smoke a blunt and talk trash, mostly about sneakers, and to throw cheap shots at Troy's new girlfriend, Big Ressa, and I'd join in. All the visits faded when Tweety started having kids, a son, followed by twin daughters. Before we were completely estranged, I asked her, "Can't y'all make it work? It always seemed like you two were meant to be."

"I love that boy, Watkins, always will," she said. "But I'm not living regular for nobody. Fuck that."

In the streets, everything is each man or woman for themself, even when we move as a team. At the end of the day, you have to take care of numero uno. It didn't matter how many sacrifices Troy would have made for her, or she for him. She was from the streets, and what it came down to was money.

Troy was crushed when she moved on. He gunned through about a dozen failed relationships, before he ultimately found love with his new lady, Jada, who was actually Big Ressa's second cousin—it was a broke love, a two hungry people sharing one Red Lobster dinner splitting a cheddar biscuit type of love, the type that no one wanted, at least not me or Tweety. It's hard to love somebody if the bulk of your time is spent surviving. The need to feed myself, and in Tweety's case her family, clouds and blurs your vision. There's no room to nurture any type of love when the quest to have dominates all. It became extremely difficult to determine who loved me or who wanted some money—so I just assumed that everybody wanted money. That was lazy, disrespectful, and unfair, but easy. Money had been the measuring stick for masculinity forever. Jesus Christ even got forked over for thirty pieces of silver, the equivalent of a couple dollars, so who the fuck was I to complain? Love was transactional.

Tweety knew I was a dog because she was a dog too. The only difference is that she accepted it and I didn't.

BOOK V

a school story

25–38 years old, 2005–2018

"You think your pain and your heartbreak
are unprecedented in the history of the
world, but then you read."
— James Baldwin

I quit. Nick begged me to stay, but I was done.

"Are you stupid?" Nick asked. "What are you going to do?"

"I'll be good."

Our neighborhood was crumbling under the weight of the drug war, and many of our friends had been arrested or murdered. I was tired of dealing, tired of everyone in my pockets, tired of feeling like I had amounted to nothing. Nick had developed a serious pill problem, popping Oxys like Tic Tacs. Everyone knew the pills were eating at him, you could see it in his graying complexion, and how his once plump face now shriveled and hung.

Then he started using heroin. The shit we sold.

One day, while strolling through the neighborhood, I found Nick, a shell of his former self. His swollen-chubby caramel cheeks were completely deflated. For the first time I could see the shape of his jawbone.

Some kids hanging around the block were poking fun at him, he was the butt of their jokes. After spotting me, Nick ran over to greet me, telling me he had this deal set up for us to hit these guys and walk away with enough money and coke for life. He was clearly delusional. I laughed and told him that I was done. He pulled a gun on me. One thing's for certain, begging and crying will not stop a trigger man from squeezing.

Nick eyed me and squeezed the trigger. I shut my eyes. The hammer clicked. I didn't flinch. I'd been there, staring down the barrel of a pistol before, but not one in the hands of one of my friends.

"Bow!" he hollered.

I opened my eyes, and it clicked again.

The gun was empty. He looked down the same barrel. "Well, damn," he said and put it in his hip. He walked past without a word, bumped me on the shoulder, and continued down the block. I could've taken the gun and beat him with it—he was in no shape for a fight—but I let him go. In 2006, about a year later, he was gunned down, murdered in a botched robbery.

———

I enrolled at the University of Baltimore at twenty-six as a street guy—I didn't think much of it, I knew I just wanted more. More of what would be discovered. I had no plan and no traditional work experience. I didn't have many friends or connections to the real world or a relationship with any person who didn't either sell drugs, punch a clock at Johns Hopkins Hospital, or clean floors for a living. I had anxiety; there was uncertainty in being a regular guy now trying to figure out real life.

To kill the extra time I now had and to escape the thoughts of what this new regular life would be, I'd read. I could be found sitting in the middle of the projects with my face stuck deep inside of a book. I found that when I read I could get through both worlds, being off the street and being regular.

I'd slip so deep and cocoon into the books that I could for the first time block out the sounds of my hood, the fighting, yelling, sirens, and even gunshots a time or two. *Pop! Pop! Pop!* "D, get down!" my homie once yelled. "They just spent the block, are you deaf?"

I had never read anything before, but I first picked up a book after a surgery I had at Hopkins as the result of a childhood injury. I was in my bed clicking through shows like *Mama's Family* and *M*A*S*H* when a young nurse—champagne-colored, with big bright sleepy eyes—walked into my room to check on me and drop off painkillers, all while keeping her nose stuck into a book. She fiddled with the machines, adjusted my drip, and took notes without even looking at me. The book eclipsed the bottom half of her face and I could only see her eyes and tiny curled 'fro peeking over her forehead.

"Damnnn, that must be a good book," I said. "I never saw a person so into a book like that."

"Oh, you'd looovvve this," she replied, not pulling her head up. "It's allllll about you."

"About me?"

"Yeah, it's a book about thugs." She looked up, and then back at the book.

"I'm not a thug," I chuckled. She laughed too, and raised an eyebrow to say, *Yeahhhh, okay.*

"So why do all of your guests have on shades and smell like pounds of weed? That is some thug behavior."

"Duh, because they got cataracts."

We both laughed.

"What was the last thing you read?" she asked, finally closing her book and giving me painkillers, which made me instantly woozy.

"Nobody ever asked me that before," I said, sitting straight up, trying not to fade. "Maybe *48 Laws of Power?*"

"Typical!" she blurted, passing me water. "Every nigga say they read that wack-ass book full of obvious lessons. You didn't read that!"

"You're right," I laughed, holding my stomach. "I own like two copies, though, you can hold one."

"Whatever," she giggled. "I'm good, baby."

When she left, I quickly dozed off. When I woke up in the middle of the night, a worn copy of Sistah Souljah's *The Coldest Winter Ever,* a novel about the beautiful daughter of a drug kingpin caught up in the game, was on my bedside.

I read it in a few days, which was fast since I wasn't a reader. And let me tell you, that book single-handedly turned me into one. An understanding I never knew I needed crept into me and grew with each page, each paragraph, each line that I consumed. A new understanding of the streets and why it had such an impact on me, of what it is to be poor, Black, and a boy in America, and how society punishes you for that. It made me think of my father and why he experienced the same pain as me, and how my future children would too if I didn't change.

I read it again and again, taking more away from it each time. The way the main character, Winter Santiago, mastered the ills of the drug game, and how it affected her family, reflected the cycle I was caught up in for so many years—the money I flaunted, the flashy, fiery kind of women I rolled with, and the love I disconnected from in order to survive, because like Tweety said, I treated everything like it was "transactional," and was only able to gauge relationships through the lens of survival.

For the first time, I was thinking critically about my life.

Critical thinking is a key ingredient in learning how to make good decisions and develop your own ideas. My entire vision for life had been wrapped around someone else's ideas. It was at this point that I realized I was living what society thought my life should be as a Black man from my neighborhood, but I didn't have to. Sistah Souljah gifted that to me. Suddenly I had a superpower, to imagine what I could be, and the confidence to really give it a try.

I read all of Sister Souljah's books. I then read every writer she ever referenced in an interview or who I thought she might have read. That put me on a path to discovering the brilliant language of Toni Morrison, James Baldwin's exceptional insight, and the genius that was Zora Neale Hurston. I also started to read through my local publications, the *Baltimore Sun*, *Baltimore Brew*, and *City Paper*, to hear from local writers and learn about other elements of our city that I'd ignored or just hadn't cared about because they didn't care about people like me.

The Coldest Winter Ever led me to *Clockers*, by Richard Price, the novel that director and producer Spike Lee made into a film. That led to *Native Son* by Richard Wright. I despised Bigger Thomas, dreaming and scribbling out the many different ways I would have conducted myself in his world of racism and limited opportunity. I wouldn't have stuffed that dead body in the furnace; I wouldn't be out drinking with the boss's daughter, and if I saw her drunk, I would've minded my business. Bigger was as nutty as squirrel shit, I'd tell my homies. That led to Ralph Ellison's *Invisible Man* because I was talking about it with a clerk at the bookshop near my house; that challenged me to read *Naked Lunch*, by William S. Burroughs, a book with loosely connected vignettes that follow an addict from Mexico to the United States, which challenged my thoughts on what I had done every day, and the author was writing from his experience; and *On the Road*, by Jack Kerouac, a book about him and his friends traveling across the country to a backdrop of jazz and drugs, which had some of the craziest sentences I'd ever seen. "But you can go on thinking and imagining forever further and stop at no decisions to pick up a bag for the thinkings. Turn your thinking into your work, your thoughts a book, in sieges."

I went deeper and deeper in the book game, expanding past America and burying my head in Russia, sitting on Ashland Avenue circling passages from *The Idiot*, by Fyodor Dostoevsky.

"*The Idiot?*" Troy asked, looking at the cover of my book. "Fuck is that about, and how can a book so big be called idiot?"

"It's a love story about a prince, who has a rep for being an idiot," I said, not looking up from my page, just like the nurse that had changed my life. "Shit is wild, we all play the fool at one point or another—you especially with chasing Tweety."

We laughed.

"Damn, man, you really hooked on reading now, that shit is kinda inspiring. Books make me sleepy."

"You ain't find the right ones yet," I said. "You should start with *The Alchemist*, by Paulo Coelho, it's short, brilliant, and it will give you a good rundown on perspective, purpose, personal legends, and omens and shit."

"Personal legends? Omens? Nigga, you gone full nerd," Troy chuckled. "You used to say I was the nerd on the computer tip, you got me now, bro."

I started making friends with many people who hung out in the bookstores around town, and they sniffed out my hunger to learn and then fed me more books to read. I kept finding the right books over and over again—books about Black men, powerful Black women, our shared history, and the legacy of Black people. I grew tied to books for my survival, stronger than any pistol I'd ever held. I thought about the anger and rage that festered inside of me. For years, I buried this anger deep inside of me with the lies. I'd always thought I was a good guy because I didn't cheat in life—not on women or in money. But I was living in self-preservation mode and blocking out any sort of relationship or personal connection that came my way so the true me wasn't discovered and exposed. I never let anyone in fully, not men and especially not women.

I was reading all about people's paths to understand what was happening with me internally. Then I read *All About Love*, by bell hooks. She forced me to look at my relationships through the lens of the trauma I had endured. "The wounded child inside many males is a boy who, when he first spoke his truths, was silenced by paternal sadism, by a patriarchal world that did not want him to claim his true feelings." I felt that, so much that I dropped the book, then picked it back up. "To be loving we willingly hear the other's truth, and most important, we affirm the value of truth telling. Lies may make people feel better, but they do not help them to know love."

Everything Tweety said to me long ago started to make sense—even my love was a lie.

I decided to change it. I had wined and dined plenty of women. I had beat down men in loyalty to my brother. But I had not learned to love. Love was what these books gave to me.

Morrison, Baldwin, Sister Souljah, the stories they told, I had developed a genuine love for them, and they told me stories even if in glimpses and little pieces of their paragraphs, and in a way that showed they loved me back. I was hooked on all of these writers, but I really wanted to be like Sister Souljah. A young writer writing about the streets in a way that I was very familiar with. Sister Souljah's work made me feel like I mattered. I needed to write. I needed to be a writer like Sister Souljah.

When I first enrolled at the University of Baltimore, I had no idea what I should be studying or doing—I just wanted to get off of the streets. Initially, I chose criminal justice as a major because I was a criminal who always wanted justice. The reading inspired me to switch my major to history with a focus on the Reconstruction era. That's where I enjoyed the works of Leon Litwack, Eric Foner, and, most importantly, W. E. B. Du Bois. After three years of taking full class loads, winter classes and summer sessions, I earned a degree in history. During my senior year I applied to a PhD program at Johns Hopkins University, but was denied. I was told by an advisor that I met the qualifications for their School of Education and could get a scholarship, so the day after I graduated, I applied for a master's program in education at Johns Hopkins and was accepted. Holding the letter felt surreal—it was funny, and I laughed out loud about it because I had lived in Baltimore my entire life and never knew a single person that went to Johns Hopkins University.

I needed to tell this to a lot of people. People needed to know that a drug dealer like me could be reformed. "Reformed into what?" was my biggest question, but I started telling my homies that I was a writer now—which was always met with their confusion or laughter. "Yeah, D, I'll believe it when I see it." It didn't bother me because I felt the same, like "Yeah, sure, D"—I still needed to prove it to myself. How was I supposed to know how far such a statement could take me? I was raised by my dad Big Dwight and the streets, and though I loved both, neither had taught me such a thing.

So I purchased stacks of bullshit books on the craft of writing, how to become a better writer, how to get published, book-proposals-for-dummies kinds of books that I never finished, and I got through school by taking it one step and class at a time until I graduated. The story wasn't as big or scary as I had imagined. I discovered what no one had ever told me: that I belonged there. After graduating from Hopkins, I went back to the University of Baltimore to attend their master of fine arts creative writing program.

———

Being Black in an MFA program is kind of like being white in the Black Panther Party. And many of the students and professors spend a huge amount of their time (so much time) reminding you that you are Black without actually saying it— it's an art to it that goes like, "Your haircut is cool, I want one," or "Only you can pull those crazy sneakers off, I wish I could wear shoes like that."

It wasn't that big of a deal to me because I had been through worse and scarier things: head cracks by racist cops, ambushes from ape-strong junkies, and shootouts within arm's length of me.

"This is a list that I'm starting for people who want to read and workshop their work next week," Berry, a square long-nosed classmate, said, handing me a blank sheet of paper. I was last in the row, and no one had signed the paper. I grabbed it and printed my name in big bold letters. Berry watched from over his glasses. "I'm going to wait until the next time, my work isn't quite ready," he said, though I hadn't asked. All I knew was that I was putting myself in debt to learn how to write, was already at a disadvantage, and didn't have time to waste. What Berry decided to do didn't really involve me. I needed to write and I wanted them to read about my experiences.

Besides not knowing where to start as a writer, half the journey in the beginning was about trusting white people with my words. My homies and I from the block had our own language, our own way of life—and I didn't know shit about these people, and they didn't know anything about me. I also didn't know how the statute of limitations worked, but as I'd look around at all of these white people, all I could think about was how much they looked like federal informants, with their square flannels and the goofy frames they wore, and I couldn't figure out why so many of them carried sweaters on the warmest days—all of that screamed witness protection to me. "I didn't make it this far to be ratted on by my class-mates," I'd go home and jokingly say to my friends.

A lot of my unease being around them would have caused writer's block, but I'd drive around my neighborbood after school to get inspired, cruising all around east Baltimore's row houses. My imagination would disappear into the projects where we'd held tough card games surrounded by empty Crown Royal bottles and chicken bones. I'd move through my favorite storefronts, the small lounges we drank too much in, and by Sportsmart and the Locker Room where I loved buying Nikes as a child. These places sparked memories and became the basis for many of my stories. Seeing the city helped me to write—but drinking and talking shit with my old friends paid the biggest dividends.

"Yo, remember when they smoked Chip's uncle?" Troy asked Tweety and me one night. I hadn't been seeing them much since starting the MFA program, but I missed them like crazy. We had linked for a drink or ten at a bar near my campus. "It was soooo much blood! D, you remember?"

"You niggas got too many damn ghetto stories," Tweety chuckled. "Does it end? Watkins, you not gonna write a bunch of ghetto shit, are you? If so, I ain't readin' that shit."

"What made you think of Chip?" I asked.

"We saw him on the corner, about a block up, lookin' real bad, bro, like a stir-fried piece of shit."

I had met Chip's uncle when I was nine years old in a corner store buying candy, he was running in and out desperately begging for change. The store owner, a Korean guy, kept threatening to call the cops, but I told him to relax. "You gotta calm down, Unk," I said. "Take a walk around the block, they gonna call 12 if you keep beggin' right here."

"Just lemme get one lil dollar, shorty," he said, digging at the nothing on his face. An old church lady by the scratch-offs shook her head and said, "That don't make no sense." He was looking at me, but I could tell he didn't see me or anything else that was happening around him. He kept asking me and the other customers the same question over and over again: "Lemme get a dollar, man." A known gangsta named Wigs slid up in the store and pushed him to the floor. Wigs purchased something and left his change in the foggy glass roll-around that separates the clerks from us patrons. Chip's uncle popped up off the floor and snatched the change. It was probably a dollar or two. Seconds later Wigs flew back into the store, beating on the bulletproof glass. "Where is my fuckin' money! Give my change, bitch!"

"It was there, I put it there!" the clerk yelled, pointing to where he had left it. Wigs pulled a pistol from his waist and rammed it into the bulletproof glass, aiming at the clerk's head. "You know who the fuck you talking to?"

"That man you knocked down took your change," the old Black church lady shouted. Wigs nodded and left the store for Chip's uncle outside and blew his brains out.

"Over a dollar?" Tweety groaned.

"A fuckin' buck," I said, downing my vodka.

"After that he dug into Chip's uncle's pocket and took his dollar," Troy said. I went home and wrote about it, and it would be my first workshopped piece. It was called "One Fuckin' Buck." I wrote about how this had turned Chip from a happy kid that loved Boston Baked Beans and chocolate-covered pretzels to a heroin user, just like his uncle, always begging for cash and banging smack into his arm, thigh, and ass all times of day.

Before the professor got to my essay, I sat near the edge of a large rectangular wooden table listening to students gush about my classmate's essay on a hiking trip where exactly nothing happened. The next one was a love story between a dog and their owners, then a story about singing in a band and a disagreement amongst crew members. And then we got to my essay. The room was so quiet you could hear an ant pissing on cotton—dead silence, crickets. *Am I terrible?* I thought. *Do I sound like a stereotypical idiot?*

"Is that how it really is in Baltimore?" a big goofy curly-haired white girl asked. "I don't think so, because that's not the Baltimore I know!"

"And what Baltimore is that?" another student asked.

"I'd never visited until I moved here for this program, but there's so many quaint pubs, the harbor, and Mount Vernon museums," she said. "Baltimore is a blast."

This irked the hell out of me. Her attitude, the way she saw the world and her confidence to play the expert on something she knew nothing about, basically defines the power of whiteness in MFA programs. I would go on to endure three years of white people telling me how great their Baltimore was compared to the stories I shared in class, or not offering me any feedback at all because I wrote about things that many of the students could not relate to. They clearly related to Harry Potter, a kid wizard flying on a broom, because that always came up; however, a Black man from Baltimore was too much to understand. But I was good at handling all of the microaggressions or whatever the term is for racist fuck-shit. Dodging the narrow-mindedness of privilege was easy because I had no interest in understanding or believing in them either.

But my biggest challenge came from a professor that punished me every chance she got. Her name was Marion Winik. She was a pint-sized woman, very critical, with a very big mouth, but she could back it up with her amazing writing ability. A lot of professors like to rip your work apart solely based on their opinions, having no real-world experience or success to justify their claims. Not Winik. She had published over ten books, including one of my favorites, *First Comes Love*, won fellowships, awards, was a board member of the National Book Critics Circle, appeared on *Oprah*, and, most importantly, she made money as a writer, so when she said something I had to listen, and it didn't matter if I liked what she said or not.

"You have a compelling story and sloppy writing," Winik told me with a sarcastic smirk the first time I shopped a piece in class. When I approached her afterward, she asked, "Are you sure you want to be in this program?"

I'd come into the MFA program with the vision, hustle, ambition, and a natural ability to tell stories. To most nonliterary types I was ready—I had a knack for perfectly delivering gangster tales about Dad and my crew and hilarious asides involving Nick, Tweety, and Troy over too much vodka for my peers and regulars at whatever bar I was out drinking at. Still, I needed some more guidance from someone who better understood where I was coming from.

"Winik really tore into me," I told Dr. Koko Zauditu Selassie, or "Mama Koko," over a drink later that day. "These are my stories and my people, and she ripped my essay apart." Mama Koko, a student like me, even though she already had a PhD, was one of the only other Black people in the program. She had been in and around the publishing industry for years before I had even thought about becoming a writer, and she understood how universities and academia work.

Receiving hard and honest critiques from Winik and Mama Koko was the missing link and, in combination with my work ethic, the foundation of my new professional career as a writer. Even as Mama Koko sat there, rolling her glossy eyes at the pedestrian mistakes I made in my essay, I knew that I would walk out of that bar with the ability to better articulate the darker parts of my life for the first time through prose. For the first time ever, I actually felt like I could make an impact. I could do for Black kids what *The Coldest Winter Ever* had done for me. Being a writer from east Baltimore, that was way more valuable than the temporary joy of running the streets.

After completing undergrad and grad school twice, I set out to start my literary career. First, I needed a literary agent. It took me about five hundred queries before I got one, Barbara Poelle, with the Irene Goodman Literary Agency. And that was only the beginning of my fight. I was flat broke and still needed money for the basics—food, shelter, and Nikes— but I wasn't looking back. I wasn't going back into the drug game, and vowed to stand by that. So after being rejected by every publisher Barbara pitched my book to, and denied by every place in Baltimore where I sought employment, I figured out a diverse cocktail for survival. I was an adjunct professor, substitute teacher, freelance web designer (a skill I taught myself just to get paid to do it), and wrote articles for whoever would run my work, collecting from $25 to $150 per piece. None of these jobs paid enough on their own, but the combination kept me off the streets, and let me live out my own expectations as the man I now yearned to be.

2

I was losing the little bit of hair I had left, while explaining the cultural relevance, the brilliance of hip-hop legend Jay-Z, to my small group of mostly eighteen- and nineteen-year-old University of Baltimore undergrads from this confusing Lil Pump–Tekashi69 generation, who signed up to take my '90s Hip-Hop class. They kept calling him "that rich guy" and saying things like, "Wow, so Beyoncé's husband used to be a famous gangsta rapper too? Cool." And they'd laugh and laugh the same way they laughed when learning about my backstory, my old hustlin' days, the battles that had knocked teeth out of my mouth, chunks out of my flesh, and left me limping as I paced the board in front of them. But I had published two bestselling books and was now, well, a good citizen.

"Y'all tellin' me 4:44 wasn't the best album of 2017! If you think otherwise, I'm failing all of you!"

My phone buzzed over and over again as I laughed at them laughing at old me screaming about my old days and the soundtrack, Jay's 1996 debut, *Reasonable Doubt*. I played track 5, "Feelin' It," gave them five minutes to analyze the song, and stepped into the hallway. My big sister Monique, who is normally a texter, had called me more than one time.

I took a pause, and hit back.

"What the hell!" she repeatedly said. "The hospital is asking who makes medical decisions in the family, Dad doesn't have a will. Where are you? Meet me at the hospital as soon as you can!"

I dismissed my class and jetted down to Johns Hopkins Hospital off Orleans Street, which is about ten minutes away from campus, two minutes the way I was driving. My dad had entered the ER three months prior because his yellow feet swelled until they puffed out of his dress shoes, looking like a popped can of those cheap biscuits. That hospital visit had turned into a three-month stay—the doctors wanted to monitor him closely because he had recently received a kidney transplant, had his gallbladder removed before that, a piece of his liver removed before that, and something done to his spleen before that, all while juggling high blood pressure and diabetes. Dad was a walking doctor's appointment.

During the second month of the three months of observation, one of his thirty doctors told my sister and me that they needed to perform open heart surgery, because he had a damaged valve. My dad was shook at the idea of having his heart cut open, or another surgery in general, but we convinced him to agree to the procedure—we had to, because his doctor was really clear when he told us, "There is no other choice."

I hated that my dad was so sick, but it felt good being around him—we'd become estranged for a few years, but his pain, his ailment, and the idea of him being in need made me forget about why we weren't seeing one another, or really speaking that much. My dad didn't call, or request my assistance, I just wanted to be there with him, the same way he had pulled up for me in the past.

"Dad just had a stroke, brain hemorrhaging was what the doctor called it," Monique said as soon as I walked into the Hopkins lobby, eyes glossy, face longer than the hallways I walked through to reach her. "This just got real, real bad." Monique, who looks exactly like a woman version of me, is not the most emotional person in the world and never really cried in front of me, but on this day, for the first time I could remember, her eyes were full, a half blink away from spilling down her face.

"We'll get through this," I told her, patting her back, because we don't really hug. "We always figure it out."

Monique paced back and forth, enough to wear down the soles on her Nike track sneakers. I leaned against the wall, my face just as long as my sister's, ocean deep in thought— I had just proposed to Caron, my best friend, my muse, and the love of my life, my writing career was finally starting to move, and now I might be losing my biggest influence, the person who I wanted to celebrate these accomplishments with the most.

"Are you okay?" my sister asked.

"Yeah, I'm good," I lied. "Just thinking of how wild Dad was back in the day."

"We have a problem with the bleeding," a short, oily, block-shaped physician in oval frames said. "We still need to do the heart surgery; however, it requires a lot of heparin, which can make the bleeding in his brain worse."

"So why did it take so long? You could have done this surgery weeks ago!" I pushed back.

The doctor slipped into a long explanation of why this was the best-case scenario—all ten-syllable words of medical bullshit, while looking at his feet, the wall, and basically everywhere except at me and Monique. Eventually I zoned out. I wanted to move Dad out of Hopkins, but decided to defer to my sister.

Monique is a real daddy's girl, he could do no wrong in her eyes—and when he did wrong, she'd be the last to acknowledge it. She was at the hospital every day, organized his bills, contacted his friends, monitored his bank account, and made sure he had a life to come back to, if he made it out. Like me, my dad was Monique's initial source of joy, the guy who taught us how to live and make light out of darkness. The thought of losing him killed us.

My mom arrived at the hospital dressed in her work clothes—scrubs and sneakers like the other hospital workers. Mom, like many mothers from Baltimore, had spent most of her professional career working at Johns Hopkins Hospital. The jobs they worked included escorting patients, the gift shop, or dietary, but my mother worked in phlebotomy. Phlebotomist sounds flashy, but they mostly draw blood for lab samples. The job required a certificate and was the first natural pivot from the kitchen because it required little training and came with a small raise. Mom had been an excellent phlebotomist at Hopkins for over twenty years until she was fired due to a racist encounter with a supervisor—I never got the whole story, but she sued and won a small settlement that came with back pay and her old position. Mom declined to go back to Hopkins, got a job at another hospital, and now we were all here, at her old stomping ground, pulling for Dad's recovery.

Monique updated her on all of the new doctor's orders. Mom and Dad had been separated but not separated for years—not legally divorced, but living in different places. For a time, he lived in Colorado. When he moved back to Baltimore, he rented a house on the south side off of

Lombard Street, while she remained over east; still she was always there for him whenever he needed her.

"Look at us all together again," Ma said. Street life estranged me from my family. I didn't really go to holiday functions or do dinners or much of anything because I was so tied into the money I chased daily; however, if they needed cash, and I had it, I'd proudly drop it off—something I was taught men were supposed to do. Now that I didn't have the money to give like I used to, I had to find a new way to express love to my family.

———

Dad and I didn't talk much during the years that he lived in Colorado, if we even spoke at all—and it was my fault. I was in a bad place mentally. I had lost some money, a significant amount, about $25,000, and a close friend, Jamie, who was battling with his addiction, was the culprit. I wanted to break his arms, but the other guy, who I had got the money from, wanted to kill Jamie. I stopped him from doing it, and we settled on a good old-fashioned ass whooping. That didn't get our money back, and I still needed to get the money back. I always hated owing people anything, especially people who could kill me. I was also stressed that my house, the five-thousand-square-foot property and my dream house, was in foreclosure, I hated that.

I was broke, I hated that.

Now I was $25,000 in debt to a murderer, I hated that.

I fractured my index finger on the side of Jamie's head after slapping him, and I hated that, too.

I hated that I had to hit him. He was like family all the way up until he wasn't. I couldn't use my hand for weeks. I also hated how I made his face look, but I had to, that's how these things work. That's the stark difference between my dad and me. He hates violence and I never saw him in a fight. I hate violence too, but it's been my first response to conflict for most of my life.

Stressing over getting that money back was starting to eat at me. I didn't really know if I was going to end up with a bullet in my head—$25,000 is a lot of money. My mental Rolodex was full of people that couldn't help, people I looked out for in the past that I knew couldn't return the favor, or people my ego wouldn't allow me to call. My finger had been puffy for over two weeks, and it wouldn't heal even after ice and ten ibuprofens a day. Out of the blue, before going out of the door for some more medication, I decided to call my dad— not to borrow money, but to hear a story or get a laugh. I got the voicemail.

"Aye, where y'all Ace bands?" I asked a tall lady in a faded stretched-out CVS shirt. She pointed to the back. I bought some more Motrin and three packs of bandages. Suddenly, all I wanted was my dad. Everything about the street life was killing me.

Besides being broke, I was also in a bad relationship with a woman who I'll call The Pitcher. The abuse with The Pitcher was very physical. I didn't hit her, but she hit me with everything she could get her hands on, from the TV remote to the Lysol aerosol can, my Nikes, and her Nikes, and her aim was impeccable, she almost never missed. I'd have new scars and bruises weekly, and started lying to my friends and family about where they came from. "I fell," "I tripped," or

"I got this playing ball," I'd say, explaining the gashes she left on my head.

"Why the fuck are you so angry?" I'd ask her sometimes, as if I didn't know. But I knew. The way I ignored her feelings, how I could just mentally and verbally shut down—that hit her just as hard as the cans she pierced my head with. And maybe my nonphysical hits lasted longer. But I could only see her wrongs. She'd call me names, I would ignore her. She'd call me more names, I'd laugh. She'd hurl everything she could at me. But when I'd leave, that was her kryptonite. It was my way of inflicting the worse pain on her. I would start by leaving for an hour. I'd grab a drink with my friends to clear my head. That turned into weeks and then I'd be gone for months at a time, to LA or Texas, or, shit, I even went to Brazil.

Now I just needed to escape my life; The Pitcher, the money, and the pain that a thousand aspirin couldn't cure. I wanted to talk to my dad.

Dad was smart. I listened to him even when I acted like I wasn't—everyone did. My brothers and sister and I, we'd all gaze off into space when he talked about politics, religion, the streets, food, films—he had commentary that would go on forever. I needed that voice right now. I needed his help, and no one else's. I wanted out of the streets, out of that relationship, I wanted a break, so I called him.

"Dad, wassup," I said.

"Hey man, how you doin'?"

"I wanna come out to Colorado and hang for a bit. I found some cheap tickets."

"It really ain't nothing for you to see out here. Don't come."

That was it. He asked how my mom and the family was doing. I held the phone, listening, not wanting to respond, wondering. I was crushed but I'd never say it. *Why wouldn't he want to see me?* I couldn't say it, the only thing I could do was lie as if it didn't hurt, but it did. It hurt more than anything because that was the only person I wanted to talk to. He wasn't there, but liquor was.

Liquor became my go-to, my consultant, the sponge that absorbed all of the emotions I buried inside of myself, my comfort, the only solution. The drink allowed me to blow Dad off, the same way I learned to cut off The Pitcher or anyone else who wasn't being what I needed them to be. I did what I did best, I used violence and street shit to cover it up and make the $25K back, paid my debt, and I saved my own life. Like a man, I did what I needed to do, just the way I was taught. This is what being a man had become. You do what you have to do, without complaining or fussing, and definitely not begging for love.

———

"Are you the Watkins family?" yet another doctor asked, approaching us in the waiting room. "Mr. Watkins can have visitors now, three at a time."

I was relieved but I stayed seated. "I'll stay here," I told my mom and sister. "Caron is on her way from work."

When they were gone, I sat there alone, even my thoughts were in solitude and not sure where to go in that situation, but then Caron appeared. She walked through the double doors of the hospital, high heels clicking as always, finishing a call; she was in a butter-soft waist-length mink and carrying a huge Louis Vuitton bag. My family was going to think that she's the most glamorous woman they've ever seen. My mom would only wear heels to church, and I can't ever remember seeing my sister in dress shoes. Now I had a fiancée who glides through with pumps on a regular Monday, as if it's normal.

I had just proposed to her a few days before. We had been dating well over a year before I popped the question. She had met my parents once on a hospital visit and my sister at a Labor Day cookout, but hadn't met my brother. Caron and I were so happy, so locked into our world, it was hard to find the space to let others in.

"Hey baby," she said, giving me a hug and a peck on the lips. She traded hugs and "How are you"s with my mom and sister, who were already coming back to get me. It was funny to watch. The idea of us being a kissy-huggy-touchy-feely family is like watching stand-up comedy. Fitting an Escalade through a keyhole is easier than getting some of my family to physically show affection.

We walked as a family down a long, bright sterile hall-way toward my dad's room, past security, the nurses' station, countless doors of quiet, doors of chatter, doors of people planning, doors with weeping family hovered around the bedside, doors of uncertainty—I was threaded with fear as we walked through the ICU.

Once Dad said, "I learned a lot about fear from my brother in the fellowship." He was in the kitchen frying crab cakes, after I got stomped out by like fifteen kids who tried to steal my Jordan 8s, the Marvin the Martians—foolishly, I would've died for them. "Fear can be one of two things," he said, dabbing the grease off of his crab cake, placing it on a saltine cracker, splattering mustard on top, and then sandwiching it with another cracker. He put my crab cakes on a plate for me and started preparing one for himself. CRUNCH, I bit into the sandwich as he continued. "So fear is the worst shit. The weakest trait, and you can handle it in one of two ways. Fuck everything and run, or face everything and rise. Don't you ever forget that!"

I wouldn't.

I swallowed the fear when we entered his room. A dim TV-lit room held a collection of machines that were attached to him. Wire clasps on his fingers, monitors beeping, doctors and nurses and doctors and nurses and specialists and machine checkers and techs in and out. Caron's head rested on my shoulder, my mom and sister were glossy-eyed. I looked over Dad's frail body as he repeatedly moaned. It was the worst pain I'd ever witnessed. I wanted to stop it.

I made my way past the group of student doctors back into the hallway to breathe. On the other side of his room door, I pulled out my phone and started to scroll, anything to numb the feelings, the stress. In the room across from me, there was an Asian couple crying, squeezing each other— displaying grief.

I felt Caron watching me as I reentered the room with a pissed expression. I could tell that she was trying to think of what she could do to ease the pain stretched across my face— the kind of pain I spent years burying. "I'm good!"

"Are you okay?" she asked, my mother watching.

"Yeah, I'm fine, we just have to keep him in prayer."

I wanted to tell Caron that I was fucking terrified of losing my dad. I was terrified of a world where he doesn't exist. Caron would have teared up, the small slanted slits she has for eyes would become smaller, and she'd offer a hug and more prayer when we were alone, advising me to see a therapist.

But I didn't say anything. Once again, of course I couldn't. Dad wanted me to say that I was good. The truth is I needed therapy a long time ago. Dad started seeing a therapist when he was out in Colorado. "Changed my fuckin' life!" he'd said.

But thinking or talking about the past makes me physically ache. The present is where I belong. Since I'm a writer, people like to ask me if writing is my therapy, and I say, "Yeah!" A fucking lie. It looks like my whole body of literary work is an accumulation of trauma I suffered, endured, created, and survived. But I learned to be hyper-selective about choosing what trauma I wanted to share. I promote what I want to be promoted, and bury what I need to be buried.

Tubes in his arms, tubes coming out of his nose, tubes connected with tubes, more beeping followed by even more nurses and doctors—a cardiologist, a nephrologist, a neurologist—and they had teams of younger doctors, baby-faced physicians in training following them around, hanging on every word they said.

The entire ordeal was too much for me to watch; an overwhelming amount of anxiety swirled in my chest. The poking and prying, pulling at his arms, his ears—their fingers opening his eyes, tugging at his bottom lip, inside of his mouth. The collection of doctors instructed their students on what was wrong with my living and still fucking breathing dad, like he was some kind of human guinea pig. After countless surgeries, countless medicine, and more brushes with death than anybody I knew, Dad was still here. I shook my head, looking at him, still breathing, still somehow strong and fearless.

Monique had made a collage of old family pictures to give my dad some inspiration—a dose of memories from our past. "Look, Dad, look at these tight-ass clothes you had on!" I said to throw off Caron's concerned stare, pointing to an '80s picture of him in a thin tank top and small shorts. Monique collected the images from old pics in her phone and my mom's house. Mom's basement holds boxes and crates of photos of our family that range from the '60s until present day, and she hates when people try to skim a few—my mother probably has a million photos and can tell you where they all are. Monique had duplicated some of the old images, printed them out, and glued them to one of those huge cardboard science-fair-looking trifolds—and if my dad makes it up and out of the hospital, Mom would be keeping that too.

Her display showcased my dad in his teens, Monique in pigtails standing next to me, Mom in a Jheri curl, and my little brother Trey's sarcastic smirk. There were also snapshots of smiling aunts and drunk uncles, people in the neighborhood who were huge parts of our lives at one point, but for whatever reason we'll probably never see again. The image that stuck out to me the most was of Monique resting her head on Dad's face, while playing with a white fluffy stuffed animal. He looks happy, so she was at peace—that was their relationship.

"Heyyyyyyyy, ahh aye," suddenly Dad murmured. "Jeanieee?

"Ah, Jeanie," he continued, looking at my sister. We all laughed and surrounded his bed like, "Ayeeeee, Dad! We love you! We love you!"

"Jean..."

"No, Dad, it's me, Mo! Mom is over there!" Monique exclaimed, pointing to Mom, who had the same girlish smirk from my elementary school days when people would ask if she was my big sister.

Dad's hands moved and then lay still. They were the same hands I knew as a child, his big yellow menacing fingers that would invade my tiny nostrils picking out boogies. They looked even bigger now because he was so small from being fed through tubes. The room grew quiet. I stood over him, waiting for his hands to move. I needed his hands to move. If they moved again, I'd be alright.

"I read that music can also jog his memory, and helps people recover from strokes," Monique said.

I pulled out my phone and punched the Tidal app—and played Aretha Franklin hits. We sat around the bed listening to Frankie Beverly's *You make me happyyyyyyyy*, Luther's *Neva too much, Neva too much*, and "Solid as a Rock" by Ashford and Simpson. Dad blinked and twitched here and there. Caron and Mom started singing along—making Mo giggle, as she joined in. Me too, all off-key like, "*Before I let gooooooooooo!*"

Dad's big veiny pale hand formed into a fist and he started humming and tapping along to the beat. My eyes, my face, my heart, every part of me—smiled.

Monique, Mom, and Caron still singing and dancing, smiling nurses peeked in, watching us as we all wrapped ourselves in that small moment of recovery.

BOOK VI

a forever story

24–38 years old, 2004–2018

"I am grateful to have been loved and
to be loved now and to be able to love,
because that liberates. Love liberates.
It doesn't just hold—that's ego. Love
liberates. It doesn't bind. Love says, 'I
love you.'"

—Maya Angelou

1

After about six months of rotating from room to room, hospital to hospital, back and forth to physical therapy, Dad finally came home. He got a second shot. We got a second shot.

He was set to move in with my mother for the first time in over ten years, and she was excited to take him in after he became ill. My mother never dated anyone during their years apart and proudly took on the difficult task of caring for a man that required countless doctor visits and physical therapy for every part of his body and the most complicated prescription combination anyone has ever seen. She never left him, I'll never know why and wouldn't dare to ask. She converted her house into a home clinic and worked around his crazy schedule while having a full-time job. Monique, Caron, and I chipped in with driving him to appointments.

"Time goes too fast," he said to me after we left one of his doctor's appointments one day. We were sitting in a sleek coffee shop. I was in and out of my chair getting us lattes and egg sandwiches and taking work calls and responding to emails, but his comment alarmed me. It sounded like he felt his was running out, which wasn't really like my dad. He was leaning back in his chair, in a multicolored Nautica fleece, dark blue jeans, and matching Pumas. It reminded me of how he used to dress my siblings and me in middle school. Looking at him reminded me of my childhood and how much I was no longer a child, but a man now.

We sat in silence until he glanced over his brown-tinted shades. "How you doin', man?"

"I'm good," I lied. I was really busy with work, work, work, and too much work. Professor, author, journalist—my schedule was out of control. And there was the wedding, it was only a couple of months away. I was about to be a married man, a husband.

And I was terrified of making the same mistakes my dad had.

Flashback to 2004

"Yo, bro, I need a favor," Tone said while looking at his phone but talking to me. "I need you to take me up Coppin." He was referring to Coppin State University. We were sitting out on Ashland Avenue. It was around noon, the part of the day where employed addicts rushed to our block to grab a midday blast. I was watching a corner man direct fiends into the alley to pull some of the attention away from our block.

"You gotta be able to read to enroll in college, Tone," I laughed, using a small rag to clean the four gold crowns that painfully hug my teeth—my grille squeezed my enamel, they were so tight it felt like my choppers were still growing inside of them. I had to wiggle them off before meals, but I liked what they did for my smile, so the torture was worth it. I pointed them up toward the sun to see how good they shone, rubbed them some more until they were spotless, and forced them back into my mouth.

"Nah, Watk, I'm not tryin' to get in school. This bitch-ass instructor up there grabbed my girl's arm or threatened her or sumtin'," Tone explained angrily, the yellow skin on his face cooking to a shade of beet red. It was hot outside but his temper was hotter. "I'ma kill this nigga!"

"Cool. Let's go!" I said. Troy was across the street working on a vision board with Tweety—they liked to cut images of resorts, jewels, and private jets out of magazines and paste them to posterboard for good luck. I banged on the door and asked them to man the fort while I went on a mission with Tone. They agreed and I headed to my truck. A smoker had just washed and waxed my Escalade till it glistened like a big black diamond. "You ready, Tone?"

"Always," he bucked back as the two of us jumped in to go to a college to assault a school employee. Cam'ron's *Purple Haze* album leaped out of the speakers, narrating our trip as we soared up North Avenue toward Coppin.

Coppin State University is one of Baltimore City's two Historically Black Colleges and Universities (HBCUs). It was founded in 1900, and eventually named after Fanny Jackson Coppin. It's a commuter school, meaning that most of the students hail from different sections of Baltimore, unlike Morgan State University, the city's other HBCU, which attracted a lot of students from New York, Prince George's County, and Philly. I'd never run up on Morgan's campus acting crazy because they had way more resources, cops, and the infrastructure to combat guys like us, but Coppin— Coppin was wide open.

"Yo, I'ma kill this nigga!" Tone screamed into his Nextel flip. "We almost there!" I shouted back, turning up the music to drown him out. Tone isn't a gangsta and never was, he's not even a little violent. He's girly-like in the face. He was timid and fragile—the opposite of everything I thought an east Baltimore man should be back then. By this time I had invested my street money into a legitimate business, and Tone was one of my first employees. We met when he wandered into my shop looking for work, telling me that he was down to do odd jobs. For me that meant cleaning my liquor store over in south Baltimore, or working as a server at my bar, or taking my cars to the shop for repairs, basically whatever I needed done that day. When we first met, he used to always tell stories about his days as a bank and credit card scammer and I'd laugh at his tales on the outside—but I always made sure I kept him as far away from my personal paperwork as possible. He did a lot for me, even things he didn't have to do, like clean my sneakers, scrub the stash house, and lie to my girlfriends when I needed an alibi. So I wanted to be there for him in the same way.

We pulled up on campus. While I was still parking, Tone jumped out of the car breathing heavy and yelling, "Where he at! Where he at!" into his phone.

I'd never seen him this mad before, cable-thick veins popping out of his shiny forehead, sweat staining the neck and pits of his shirt. I was actually starting to believe he might kill the guy. A small Black female appeared across the street from where we parked. She was in a faded denim jacket, with a long blonde streak of hair covering her eye. Tone went over to her with his arms wide open. When she turned in his direction I saw her wide belly poking out, giving a lowercase b shape. I was surprised to see the round-ness of her stomach. *Tone didn't tell me she was pregnant*, I thought. This was why he was so upset. The employee didn't just disrespect his girlfriend, he assaulted the mother of his child.

Tone introduced me to his girl. I waved. We followed her to the campus studio and I can't remember exactly what she was saying, but she was as mad as Tone. All of her words came out muffled as she wiped away tears that wouldn't stop. "That bitch-ass nigga has pictures of me, I can't believe that shit!" she cried. Tone wrapped his arm around her tiny shoulder and gently kissed the side of her head.

"Relax, I'm here now baby, relax, relax..." he said, one hand rubbing her back in circular motions. She exhaled a gust of relief.

We walked across the patches of green, the tall buildings and multiple paths that made up Coppin's campus. The quad was covered in happy students posted on the manicured lawns and by the benches, and hustling back and forth. They all looked way more important than me and Tone—people our age doing something more productive with their lives than hustling and going to potentially beat up an employee. Their bright futures seemed inevitable to me, a college dropout, liquor-store-owning bum, with illegal poker machines and one foot in and one foot out of the drug game. In ten years they'd be flourishing in their important careers. In ten years we'd probably be dead.

"He's downstairs in here," Tone's girlfriend, who told me to call her Tia, said, pointing to a large glass door with rectangular-shaped handles.

Tone and I walked right into the building as if we were students like Tia, and arrived at the guy's office. I placed an ear close to the wooden door and heard voices. "A yo, somebody is definitely in there."

Tia knocked with her small brown hands that were almost the same color as the door: *Tap tap, tap.* No answer. She knocked again, lighter this time: *Tap, tap, tap.* "Yo, that's a

Mouse knock," I said. "You gotta beat on the door like the fuckin' police!"

Tone moved her to the side, looked at me, turned his back toward the entrance, and hammered his boot dead into the center like *BOOM! BOOM! BOOM!* Hard enough to splinter the door, making the wood shake.

A young woman in a sky-blue tube top that matched her high-waisted miniskirt swung the door open, pulling on her dress and adjusting her shirt over her cleavage. She paused, and then rushed out of the room past our trio.

"Baby, you ain't got to leave," the man whom Tia said had assaulted her called out.

Slap him, I thought.

"Who are you? What do you want?" the employee yelled over to us. He looked *pimpish*—from his fried hair and thin gold chain to his sharply creased seersucker-type pants and a quarter zip sweater covered in leather and suede patches woven into the knit, all seasoned with balls of lint. He patted and felt around his pockets, looking for something. I closed the door, said, "Relax, man," and walked toward him. I could see the fear clogging his pores as he · backed toward his desk. Tone's flesh turned red, Tia reached for his hand and squeezed it. The employee, still looking at me, placed a hand on the receiver of the black office phone that sat on his messy paper- and photo-cluttered desk. I yanked the cord out of the jack and dropped it into the trash can. The guy's eyes were wet, his nostrils flared to a wide bloom, with a twisted lip that made up the perfect cry face. With one hand on her belly and still holding Tone with the other, Tia screamed, "Why the fuck you grab me?!" He denied it. "What you mean, baby girl? I did no such thang!"

Slap him.

"I don't know what she's talking about!" he stuttered. "I'd never touch her, I'd never touch nobody!"

"You betta not say nothin' to her," Tone boasted, his voice cracking.

"I won't, I won't," the employee pleaded. "Please leave me be."

This greasy pimp looked old enough to be our granddad. Old enough to know he shouldn't be touching young girls, or crying about it when he was caught. His pointed church shoes and musky brute smell and the constant begging and crying annoyed me, but I kept my cool, twiddling my fingers while they went back and forth.

Slap him.

Then the energy shifted. I guess he realized that Tone was never going to hit him, and then he started yelling, demanding that we leave, "Or else!"

WACCCCCCCCCCCCCCCCCCKKKKKKKK!!!!!!!! I slapped him—slapped him off his feet, slapped him into the wall, slapped him into the Friday after next, slapped some sense into him, slapped the Black off of him, slapped the change out of his pockets, slapped him so hard the palm of my hand reddened and began to sting. After dude hit the wall and the shelf next to it, he bounced onto his table, knocking down the plaques and items that sat on his desk.

"Call campus security!" he screamed out to no one.

Before I hit him again, I turned to see if Tone wanted some, but him and Tia were gone. I ran out of the office, dashing through the hallway, scrambling toward the building exit. When I looked up, Tone was right behind me, laughing. I stopped running as soon as we broke free of the building and again saw the light of day. "Yo, let's stop runnin', chill, just act like a student." He agreed, the running made us look like guilty assailants. I was sure security or the cops were already in pursuit of us for slapping the shit out of a campus employee.

And just before I saw my truck, right before I was off of campus property—a pretty brown woman with tiny eyes, the prettiest woman I had ever seen, walked across my path. She turned her head, her smile, poetry. This was Caron. I didn't know that she'd one day be my wife. I thought she probably wasn't my type; she probably had a boyfriend that went to church when it wasn't Easter, as a matter of fact he probably went to church twice a week, and they probably had a weak-ass life plan, a whole agenda including recycling, hiking, and other boring shit that had nothing to do with my lifestyle. But her smile eased me, I believed that smile would be etched into my mind until I saw her again. Armed campus security could have been on my heels, ready to lock me up for what I had just done, but I was stuck on her. It was just a small glance but my heart stopped. We didn't lock eyes and I didn't stop to introduce myself, but everything in front of me paused.

"Come on, Watk!" Tone pushed, yanking my arm.

Tone and I made it back to my truck and pulled off. Tone immediately jumped on his phone to brag to our crew about how I'd slapped the guy. We cruised back down North Avenue, toward my strip, and I cranked up the music to drown him out. I was silent as we floated back to where we belonged, unable to think about anything but that smile.

2

"Yo, bro, I know you don't fuck with clubs, but bro, come to the premiere of a film with me," my friend Day Day asked one day while we were driving around, sharing a blunt and ideas. "Get a drink or three, it's gonna be some girls there!" he added, adjusting his flat cap. I always hated those hats. The kind of hat dudes wore who said things like, "Jazz ain't what it used to be." But Day Day could pull it off with his crisp button-up shirt, with both sleeves evenly rolled up. He was always fly. Day Day was also a great basketball player from Chapel Hill Projects who introduced me to the idea that a dude could be from the hood but still do artistic things like make films and practice photography.

"Shit prolly gonna be goofy, bro," I said, "but I'll roll." I was tired from taking a full load of graduate courses; however, a night out every once in a while didn't hurt.

Day Day was a producer and an actor. He had roles in a few movies and rap videos, including *Dead Money*, which was premiering that night. *Dead Money* was an indie film about a group of drug dealers who murdered people just to steal their organs and sell them to rich white people on the dark web who were looking to extend their lives. A bunch of other dudes from Baltimore were in the film, and it was starring

Next Friday's star, Clifton Powell. Powell's not a Denzel-level A-list celebrity, but he was to us. He'd been in another of our favorite movies, *Menace II Society*, and a bunch of other hood classics we loved, so a dude who in our eyes "made it" in the industry hanging with us at a nightclub in Baltimore was kind of a big deal.

"What you wearin', bro?" Day Day asked.

"What I got on." I shrugged, surveying my fit. Black Jordan 3s, still my favorite shoes ever since Ant slid to the corner with them that day, some gray Nudie jeans, a classic red and black flannel, a black overcoat, and a Burberry scarf.

When we arrived, I slowly walked behind Day Day into the crowded club.

"They gotta table for us upstairs," Day Day told me. "We not buying any drinks!"

"Cool, cuz I'm broker than my iPhone," I replied, showing off my cracked-up screen. We cut through the dance floor, dapping homies, people grabbing me, making introductions and saying, "I haven't seen you since..." as we approached the VIP section.

I surveyed the room and immediately knew I didn't belong there. Everyone was in fancy shoes or cheap versions of what looked like fancy shoes, champagne flutes were being passed around by respectable Black men in cable-knit sweaters with big dumb drunk smiles. Everybody was dressed in their best church clothes to see this film, except me. Day Day had hard bottoms on, but this was normal for him—he liked to wear sneakers too, but brunch boots or oxfords didn't make him feel strange. I could never wear church shoes—even the expensive ones feel flat, awkward, and slippery as a Chicago sidewalk in January. I was looking around, knowing that I was underdressed, and sticking out like a sixth toe.

And then I saw that smile again. The grin of grins, delicately painted on that beautiful face.

She was dressed like she worked at an office or something—shirt, jacket, and blouse all courtesy of "the Hillary Clinton Line," if such a thing existed. She was sitting next to a homely-looking dude in a dry sweater. Instantly I didn't care about going to sit in VIP with no damn Pinky from *Friday*, fuck him, I wanted to sit next to her—but she looked friendly with the guy, so I needed to get a sense of what "they" were so that I could properly infiltrate. Their body language screamed friend zone. If she was with me, my arm would've blanketed her shoulder. I smelled friend, not lover. I'm the lover.

"Gimme a second, bro," I told Day Day, "I'ma go get this girl real quick. I'll meet up with y'all in a lil bit!"

"Yo, see if she got a friend—" Day Day was saying as I walked off.

"I got you," I spat back.

Maybe she was in a relationship with the sweater dude, and they had a big fight and that's why he was not touchy with her. Maybe she didn't like his sweaters, maybe he cheated on her and got caught fucking the girl from the ugly sweater store. I didn't care. I walked up to her, introduced myself, and asked her name.

"Caron," she said and then turned back to the screen where they were showing Day Day's movie. Fuck that movie, I needed her attention.

"This movie is terrible," I said, chuckling. "I read the script!"

She shot me a dirty look. "My friend worked on this film."

I didn't know if it was the dude sitting next to her or someone else. He must have felt her energy, like I was annoying her, so he stepped in, saying, "Yo, what's up," in an aggressive tone.

If I was ten years dumber I would've immediately cracked his jaw in half for speaking to me like that. But I'm off the block, I'm semi-educated, I'm relaxed now. "What's up, brother," I replied with a big smile. "You guys sure look like you are having a good time, man. I would love to join you two."

Once he realized that I wasn't trying to be a threat, though I was, he started talking about the film, the art he loved, his birthday, and all kinds of things I didn't care about. I pretended to listen to him, acted interested, nodded with wide eyes in excitement as he continued. *She can't be with him*, I thought. *If so, she may need me more than I need her—he could potentially kill us all with boredom.*

When he'd take a breath, I'd slip in some jokes. She wouldn't laugh.

"Yo, grab us some drinks, get whatever you want," I said to her friend, handing him my card, knowing my bank balance was under $120 and it had to last until the end of the week. But I could look at his sweater and tell he wasn't the sort to spring for a bottle of champagne—it'd be a beer for him and house wine for her at best.

Dude left us alone and I used the opportunity to learn everything I needed to know about Caron. She worked for the comptroller's office, she was in law school, had a master's degree, a sister, lived in east Baltimore but was from west, owned a small ugly dog that she showed me a photo of, and loved sock monkeys and red wine. Her smile was even more beautiful up close.

I told her that I was a writer. I was just starting to get comfortable with that, because I didn't really know what that really meant as a livelihood, or if it was going to work out. This was the part where people would laugh or tell me to get a real job, but Caron was intrigued.

"Send me some of your work," she said.

"Of course."

Sweater dude came back with the drinks. He slipped right back into the conversation where he'd left off. We all laughed and probably did another round or two. I played it all well, and then I pulled out my phone, hiding the severely fractured screen from dropping it so much and not having the money to replace it, and I got her number. Mission accomplished.

"Who is that, bro?" Day Day asked as we exited the party. "What's up wit her?"

"I dunno," I said, "but she lookin' like her last name should be Watkins."

"Word." He nodded.

"Yeah, she bad as shit, and smart."

I texted her that night but didn't hear back. I texted her again the next day. Nothing. A couple more times but she never really hit back. When she did, it was vague, like the text you send your grandma to avoid long conversations. She really wasn't interested in me, and I didn't really mind—because again, I was broker than my phone screen.

3

I gave up on connecting with Caron, and then one day she reached out.

My phone buzzed across the table. I couldn't believe her number was flashing across my screen, which was fixed now. I was sitting in front of a Thai restaurant on Preston Street, having a drink with a friend. My day was rough, shit, I was having a rough year, and her call made me feel better. I was in between two or six failed relationships— the woman I was currently leaving had just called me "a broke son of a bitch who can't write." bell hooks's book *All About Love* taught me to let people in emotionally; however, she never explained that opening my heart and sharing my deepest and most personal secrets gave women the space to call me a "broke son of a bitch who couldn't write."

I was unemployed and my money issues were worse than they had ever been. I was so broke that 99-cent ramen noodles were a delicacy—I ate at noon so that my hunger wouldn't come back till seven. Troy had gotten stabbed in the neck, but survived, and two of our best friends were part of a huge federal indictment—but now, randomly, this woman with her fancy state job who had been totally out of my league was reaching out to me. It felt like a sign that good times were to come.

She said she'd just ridden past the restaurant and saw me.

"I'm going to Hopkins to study," she said. "You want to come by and keep me company?"

I told her that I wouldn't rather be anyplace else in the world and hopped in my car.

She asked me to bring her some snacks, including a bag of plain Utz chips and some Sour Patch Kids. Since I overdo everything, I bought her a bag of chips and a pack of Sour Patch Kids, and I got five of each, before blasting off to the university.

I thought about telling her about the first time I saw her, but I didn't want to scare her. I figured that I should just let her talk, she'll create the vibe, I thought.

"I can't eat all of this!" Caron laughed, twisting her soft lips.

We sat alone in the library and she told me about law school, and working for the comptroller, and when she danced in Paris as a child, and her love for Jesus. Jesus was her homeboy, literally. She *really really really really really really* loved Jesus.

I listened, chiming in about art and writing and business ideas. I didn't tell her that I was struggling, frustrated, and some weeks barely made enough to eat—oh, and a few of my best friends, who I haven't seen in a few years, may be going to federal prison, and how I may be joining them, if they decided to drag me into their shit. She made me forget about all those things.

I gave her a screenplay I was working on about two east Baltimore basketball stars, ripped apart by jealousy and fame. She put it in her bag as we left the library.

"It's so good!" she said to me on the phone a few days later.

"There's so many typos, I corrected them all, but it's so good."
She even started asking me questions about the plot.

The women I dated would say they read, or would read,
but then when I asked them about it, they'd say things like,
"I'm busy, keep writing, you are gonna be so good one day,"
and my favorite, "I love that you write, that is so different!"
But they never bothered to ask about it.

Caron reading what I wrote and just being Caron stole my
heart. She was so sweet, kind, the type of person that seemed
like she would give her last to someone she cared about. Plus,
she was drop-dead gorgeous—too gorgeous, when she dressed
up or down, too gorgeous for me.

We started talking all the time, multiple times a day, slowly
developing our own little world—filled with stories we both
knew the endings to, told in a special dialogue that only the
two of us could understand. This went on for weeks.

We'd meet up for drinks at this cruddy basement dive bar
called Dionysus with sticky red couches that smelled like
Febreze spritz over ass, drunk patrons and drunk staff who
drank more than they worked, and menus full of bland dishes
that were perfect for soaking up the alcohol we consumed. If
we weren't shutting the bar down, we'd get together after she
was done studying, normally around 11 p.m. when I'd watch
her fall asleep in restaurants or in the passenger seat of my car.
We developed a friendship—an I-really-like-you, I-could-see
myself-with-you type of friendship.

One night we stopped at 7-Eleven before heading down to
the waterfront to one of our favorite parks, and we bumped
into a friend of hers, a pleasant portly dude named Miles.
He was frantically pacing back and forth so quickly he could
have put a hole in the ground.

"Miles, is that you? I'm not used to you being dressed

down," Caron said, walking into a hug. "He's normally dressed all the way up," she said to me and introduced us.

"I'm sorry, guys, my phone is dead, I'm locked out of my house," Miles said. "I can't find my landlord. This has been the worst day of my life."

"Can you help him?" Caron asked me.

"Of course I can," I said proudly.

I'm not a mechanic or crack-a-lock kind of guy, but I could not let her think that there were problems in the world that I couldn't solve—so I checked my trunk, grabbed a flathead screwdriver, and we made our way to Miles's crib. As we drove over, I listened as they reminisced about their wild party days and types of things I missed out on as a consequence of choosing the streets in my formative years. I liked listening to their stories. It kind of made me wish I was a square, with my biggest issue as a teen having been picking an outfit for a party.

We arrived at Miles's crib, a quaint row house that looked identical to the spot me and Troy stashed work in, except it was on an expensive side of town in a white section of Baltimore.

"Yo, y'all look out for cops and nosy neighbors because we are in Canton," I said to Caron and Miles. They agreed, sliding back to give me my space and keep a lookout. I also didn't want them on my back while I tried to crack his lock. I'm not handy and I never was a thief, but I busted into my fair share of homes to collect debts or whatever. Having that skill automatically makes you look sketchy, so I could only imagine what Miles and Caron were thinking.

Is he a criminal? Does this guy spend his free time breaking into houses?

Miles's door was made of steel and extra sturdy. There

weren't any gaps or screws on the front of the door, and it was sealed too tight for me to crack it with my shoulder.

While I was thinking, a spindly white man dressed in flannel and burning a cig approached us. "I can help you get in there. I can break into anything. I'm from Dundalk."

Caron and Miles looked scared.

"Get over here, Dundalk," I laughed. "Let's do a B&E."

Dundalk is predominantly a white lower-class community on the outskirts of Baltimore—those white boys listen to rap, ride dirt bikes, and flip on cops just like we did in the city; they even wore Timbs and exclusive Nikes like us. We kind of spoke the same language, they were just white.

I stood near the knob, giving Dundalk the space he needed to access the lock. He pulled out a credit card and slid it between the door and the lock. "When I say go, you push that fucker," he told me. "Not a light push, really shove this fucker."

In about a minute, Dundalk said, "Go!" and I pushed the door but it didn't click. Dundalk stood back, scratching his head—then we traded the card back and forth in a crooked dance, both trying to pop the lock.

"Wait a second," Dundalk said, pulling out another card. I got out my screwdriver, and as he slid the card in and caught the lock, I jammed in the screwdriver and we popped the door wide open. Miles and Caron jumped for joy, praising us as their heroes.

"Motherfucker!" Dundalk yelled as we high-fived.

"You guys wanna come in for a drink?" Miles asked, his mood lighter now.

"I gotta jet, bro," I said. "Next time we'll do a round."

"I'd love to, Miles," Caron said, "but I should leave with him. It was great seeing you..."

As I drove home, I could feel Caron's eyes trained on me hard, a blinkless stare floating over her smile. It was the biggest smile in the world. I didn't know if she was just happy we got Miles into his house or if watching me bust all manly-like into her friend's home was making her fall for me. It turned out to be the latter. She cut through all of the bullshit and asked me to be with her, not in a direct way but in a "What are we doing?" type of way.

"I got a lot going on," I told her, pulling up to her house. "A whole lot happening, and I can't think about a relationship right now."

Her eyes watered, and then she looked at me in disgust, before leaping out of my car, vowing to never see or talk to me again. I called after her as she ran off, making one of those dramatic TV exits, entering her house and slamming the door. I couldn't tell her everything that was going on with me, about being broke—that was embarrassing—and recovering from a trash relationship I had blown so many good years on, how no literary agent would sign me, and that I was burned out on trying to live a regular life.

She made me happy at a time when I couldn't return the favor, and I didn't want to mix her up with my shit. I spent my whole life buying things, committed to the notion that those things would eventually make me happy. They never did. Caron deserved more, and I loved her. I really loved her too much for her to be with a guy like me.

I sat in my car for a while watching her door, wondering if she'd notice and come back out. She never did.

4

It was sticky, hotter than fish grease, two thousand degrees outside, or at least it felt like it. I was leaning on a wall near 35th Street in northeast Baltimore.

"Okay, D, we need you to stand right here and look into this camera," Theo, the camera guy said, angling my shoulders. "Explain the history of segregation in this Baltimore neighborhood."

I squeezed the mic, wiped the sweat off of my brow again, and talked about racism again, segregation again, redlining again, and blockbusting again—for the third time.

"I'm exhausted by trauma talk, bro."

Theo and his girlfriend, Sara, were freelance directors and videographers who had sold some work to Vice. They both read the "Too Poor for Pop Culture" essay I had published and thought I would be a great host for a television show. They wanted to pitch me to Vice. That essay had brought me all kinds of attention from producers and TV personalities who had the same kind of idea, even though I had no experience in television.

At first, I thought I could be the subject of some wild and crazy Cinderella story, "Dope Boy from the Hood Makes It Big in Hollywood!" But after producer after producer had me running to New York for pointless meetings or filming myself for hours before ghosting me or telling me that the studio said no at the last minute, I just figured it wasn't my time and that I should be focusing more on my books. I loved writing, and writing opportunities were now finding their way into my inbox every day. But Sara and Theo were different, they had good ideas and it was fun to hang around them, so I gave them a shot. We were filming me giving commentary on neighborhoods. I hung in these areas so it wasn't the worst way to spend a day.

So here I was, baking in the sun, talking Baltimore racism in my raw unfiltered voice. This street was our third stop. Earlier that day we hung with Nicky, the coolest young boy from my neighborhood, who happened to be a squeegee kid; and at a peace rally for McKenzie Elliott, a three-year-old girl who was killed by a stray bullet.

"There's a rec center called Collington Square that is detaining kids for this new curfew law," Theo said. "I heard it's like a baby jail!"

"Come on, D, one more stop?" Sara begged. "If we can get in there, capture your reaction to seeing kids detained, then this doc will sell for sure!"

"Okay, okay," I responded, wiping more sweat off of my shiny forehead. "One more stop."

Night fell on us as we pulled up in front of the rec. I was finishing a piece of blunt that I'd been taking tokes off of all day, allowing the smoke to mellow me out in preparation for this last segment. Day Day had joined our trio, passing me a bottle of cologne as I exited the car. I sprayed the funky weed smell with YSL and made my way to the rec door—Day Day, Theo, Sara, and their camera behind me.

I knocked on the door.

A sheepish dude answered with a light voice, "Can I help you?"

Sara stepped to the front, as she had been doing all day because people tend to respond better to white women. "Hello, I hope your day is going well, we are with Vice and working on a film about the new curfew law."

He looked us all up and down, one by one.

"We would like to get in to talk to some of the detained kids," she said.

"We aren't detaining kids," dude said. "I can let you in but let me get the lady from the mayor's office. They are in charge."

Theo's eyes lit up in excitement. Sara started jotting down potential questions and talking points.

"I go off the cuff, Sara," I laughed. "I don't do talking points."

Dude cracked the door and pointed at us. "This is the Vice TV crew."

Caron walked out behind him. *Beautiful as always*, was my first thought. She was in fitted business attire and looked annoyed when she saw me but then graced me with that smile. Sara and Theo began making their case—but I knew Caron, she was too sharp and smart to be persuaded or bullied.

"Hey, back off, give us a sec," I told the crew, while pulling Caron to the side.

Caron had left her job at the comptroller's office to run communications for the mayor—always ambitious, always climbing up the financial ladder.

"I miss you," I said, pausing for a reaction. None. Finally, I said, "You gonna let us in?"

She shot me a look that said, *You-must-be-outta-your-goddam-mind-if-you-think-I'm-letting-you-in-here-with-a-camera*. I knew

I had a permanent spot on her bad side, but took a crack at her anyway. "This is a cool production. We are just showing love from both sides, and we really can't do it without your help. Will you help an old friend out?"

"Sorry," she said, "it's too much happening and now is not the time."

After giving me the dagger, she smoothly walked right back into the center.

"What the fuck is her problem?" Theo asked.

"I know what her problem is," Day Day laughed.

"Am I missing something?" Sara asked.

"Nah, that's my baby..."

5

My first book, *The Beast Side*, dropped in September 2015. This is when I was a *New York Times* bestseller and a big deal. I was featured in all of the local newspapers in Baltimore and had some DC write-ups too. Things were really looking good for me—I got some good leads on a couple of jobs and people were starting to pay me to speak. I hadn't felt this confident since my street days, but instead of squandering my new earnings on $10,000 vacations and spilling champagne like water, I saved all of my money up, and only treated myself to new Nikes. I was attending lunch meetings with "well-connected" people. I was the hottest guy in town, and they all wanted a piece. I also wanted to pick their brains, so that I could learn what I needed to know about Baltimore business and how to legitimately flip the little bit of money I had now.

Most of the meetings were pointless. Mainly political scammers telling me how cool they used to be and how they will make Baltimore better through policy. But they all weren't bad, some of the meetings were entertaining. I'd talk for many hours with these old dudes at my favorite restaurants, teaching me things about food and dishing the dirt on love triangles between local politicians, news personalities, and other notable people. I was always taught that gossiping is for *suckas,* so I never commented or repeated what I heard, but it was good to know that the rich people were just as messy as us regular people.

I kept getting invited to all kinds of offers to join campaigns, which I declined, but I did attend one launch party for a city council member. He had his eyes set on being mayor, but I didn't care—I went for one reason and one reason only. Caron. I heard that she might be attending the event so I gladly pulled up.

It was a typical party where I spent most of my time repeatedly saying "Thank you" to people who congratulated me on the book as I sipped cheap box wine, trying not to look awkward. A guy who told me he was a developer started giving me his life story, and I had to respectfully ask him to put a pin in it because Caron walked by.

She spotted me. I couldn't tell if she was happy to see me or not. She kind of flipped her hair and looked away to greet some suits. *I'll wait for her to finish,* I thought, *I'll say hello, and then I'll leave.*

A few minutes later she made her way over to my section, cheap wine in her hand too, wearing that smile and the latest in the Hillary Clinton Line. My heart stopped.

"Hey, superstar," she teased. "Everybody is talking about D. Watkins this and D. Watkins that, and I be like, *puhlease.* Whatever. I once knew that clown."

"Oh, you still know me?"

We laughed, then she congratulated me on all of my success. I congratulated her on finishing law school, passing the bar, and landing the new job. After all, I had con-tributed with the snacks. These days she had made a name for herself as one of the sharpest communications experts in town.

"You know I reached out to you, right?" I said, taking a heavy swig of the cheap wine.

"No, you didn't," she laughed. "You don't have to lie."

"I sent you a poem!" I said, scrolling through my phone looking for the text.

She said, shuffling through apps, that she didn't receive it.

I found it and sent it again.

It read (bear with me, I'm not a poet):

I think I fill you
Mentally
And physically
Maybe feel you spiritually

*

Either way I'm your perfect mistake
Your perfect mistake
You should've walked away

*

Ignored me, blocked me, canceled the date,
But I'm your perfect mistake

*

We are connected by colors that don't exist, painted on
    untouched walls is a foreign place drenched in
    incomprehensible love that can't die

"Ohhhhh," she said, suddenly remembering. "You are on my blocked list. I blocked you."

"Whattttttttt!"

We laughed, and I offered to walk her to her truck since

the event was ending. She hadn't purchased my book, so I asked if she wanted a copy.

"Write me a special note," she said. "Don't write something that you wrote for one of your girlfriends."

I wrote:

Caron,

You are too perfect for me, but seeing your smile again makes me think about the time I was lucky enough to be a part of the magic you are—you are so smart, beyond beautiful, I'm grateful to be able to call you my friend,

Love,
D

Caron and I may not have realized it but, as I had hoped, walking her to the car meant walking back into each other's lives. This time I vowed to be the man I wanted to be for her.

———

As the year rounded out, when we weren't together, we were talking on the phone or texting. And that turned into little dates, day dates, dates to plan dates, and overnight dates. Our connection was a dangerous addiction for us both, but especially me—we turned into the kind of friends who acted more like a couple than friends.

One day, we got into a crazy fight when she saw me getting out of another girl's car in front of the train station near my house. It wasn't a date, a love interest, or anything like that—just a random lady I knew who was going through a difficult time and needed some advice. She wasn't my type, and I was honestly just killing time until Caron was free. I was free, wanting to get drunk, so I invited her out for a drink, but it was late, and everything in Baltimore closes around 2 a.m., so she slid by my house around 3 a.m. Single people can do what they want. She came by my apartment and we smoked and drank until I had to get a train to New York around 7 a.m. Caron saw us from where she was secretly spying across the alley and lost her shit.

"Whose car were you getting out of?" she screamed into her phone, so loud that I had to pull my phone away from my ear.

"What?"

"You heard me!"

She was angry at what she saw, and I was angry that the incident bothered her enough to question me. So like a dummy, I deflected.

"You can't question me, we're not even together," I said. We yelled back and forth and then I slipped back to my old self and lied, "An Uber, I got out of an Uber."

She was smart enough to know that wasn't an Uber, and I didn't even know why I lied. Why would I lie about something that I shouldn't even be lying about? *What the hell is wrong with you*, I kept asking myself. The fight scared me. The thought of losing her was terrifying. I called her from New York and apologized, over and over again—and came back home as fast as I could. She forgave me and agreed to meet me at my place to talk.

While I was sitting alone in my apartment waiting for her, I kept looking at the door every five minutes and checking my watch. *Did she say five minutes or five hours?* I thought. Either way, she was taking too long, a second felt like a year, and I was getting mad—anxious. I wanted to be around my friend, I wanted to make sure we were good and to let her know that I would never make her feel like that again. *Where was she?*

I had things to tell her. I needed to explain myself. I realized that something in me had shifted. I felt different. I had all these feelings that I wanted to share with her immediately. And at the same time, I just wanted to hear about her day. And in that moment, while waiting for her, I realized that I needed her. That I had let myself need someone. That I wanted to tell her everything from the stories about the people I hurt, people who hurt me, my strengths, my weaknesses, and even the reason why I was thirty-eight years old and still tended to pull my eyelashes out. That she crept in and shattered the steel wall that housed my emotions.

Fuck.

I was so in love—I could really be a square for her, I really loved Caron, and I told her. And this time, I asked her if she wanted my heart, knowing who I am, and bet her feelings on who I could grow to be.

She said yes, and just like that I was loved.

6

It was raining like crazy outside. I was sitting in my car in front of Smyth Jewelers, located in Timonium, on the outskirts of Baltimore City. It was one of the few places in Baltimore that had a ring good enough for Caron, who was elegant and extremely flashy. I walked into the store dripping with water, prepared to dump my whole net worth on a diamond.

I already knew what kind of ring to buy—a few months prior, Caron and I took a trip to San Francisco, and while walking down Market Street taking in the sights, we popped into a jewelry store.

"Hey, baby, try on some rings," I said, and I didn't have to say it twice. Caron found a comfy seat and the happy money-hungry salesman pulled out some of his best merchandise. Her tiny fingers were greased and ready.

Caron and I weren't talking about getting married at that time, but the day I saw that ring made both of us imagine the next step a little more. It was platinum with an emerald rock the size of a baseball. It was perfect. I loved that ring, it looked so good on her finger, as good as the smile she made as we both admired it.

"How much is this ring?" I asked. The salesman took it

off of her finger and examined the small tag attached to the bottom.

"This one is $100,000," he said. We both laughed.

"Try it on again, baby," I said. She put it back on and hand-modeled it. I took a picture of it and made it a favorite in my phone.

A couple of men walked past me in Smyth like, "Hey, can I help you?" and I just waved them off. Then I was confronted by a short saleswoman named Luca, who was covered in nice jewelry and seemed like she knew her stuff.

"Yes," I said, "I'm looking for an engagement ring."

Luca led me into a back office, where they served me wine I did not drink and snacks that I did not eat. You should never make business decisions while drunk. She taught me why some of the smaller diamonds were way more expensive than the bigger ones. "It's all in the cut." I spent hours looking at rocks, dozens, in search of the right one. After I found it, Luca helped me customize a ring, similar to the one Caron modeled in San Francisco. When everything was perfect, I left the store and came back with a wad of cash.

"We take credit," Luca said.

"This works for me," I replied, separating the stacks of 100s and 50s.

It only took them about a month to get the ring together, and it was perfect. Now I needed to figure out how to pop the question.

I couldn't believe that I had bought a ring for Caron to marry me. I thought about that first time I saw her on Coppin's campus. I thought about Tweety—she would have been proud. She was right about me having the ability to be better, different than I had ever imagined I could be.

Caron's mom, Cherlyn, loved me, so I texted her on the day I picked the ring up, inviting her and Caron's dad, Mike, out to dinner to get their blessing.

Caron had a great relationship with her parents. They're progressive, cool, and educated. She was raised in the church and in a single-family home. She took ballet lessons, ate vegetables every day, even went to Disney World more than once. While Caron was in church taking communion and learning the Lord's Prayer, I was cutting school, instigating fights, and then there were the murders I witnessed at five, eight, and nine. None of that mattered tonight, though, because I was in a beautiful angelic place with good people, professing my love for an extraordinary woman, and able to leave the pain of the past behind to live my future.

I met her parents at Ida B's, a soul food restaurant. It was packed, with a long wait, but I knew the owners and they found me a table without a reservation. I sat there and patiently waited for Caron's parents.

"Please order whatever you want," I said when they arrived. "Even if it's not on the menu."

I knew the chef hated that, but I was trying to make a good impression and I could make it up with my tip. A slow silence wrapped the table, but soon enough we were turned up like old friends, sharing stories about Caron, who we all loved so much.

"I always thought she would be too bossy to get married," her dad joked.

"Oh, she is bossy," I added. "But I love it."

Then I pulled out the ring. They loved it. They were so happy and so was I. When I exited the restaurant, I realized that I didn't need a big extravagant proposal with singers and a video crew, all I needed was the two of us.

The rain came down harder on my windshield as I drove home. I dialed Caron, and she answered. "Hello?"

"Hey, baby, can we hit the waterfront tonight?" I asked.

"It's a mess out there, but my hair isn't done, so okay."

I pulled up in front of the water. She jumped out of the car laughing and dancing and playing in the rain like a goofball. I followed. With her back facing me, she kept strolling ahead. "Why are we here tonight?" she asked, laughing. And then she spun around and I was on one knee, with the box open.

Tears exploded from her eyes like a broken faucet, as I, the boy from east Baltimore, professed his love.

She said yes.

BOOK VII

a family story

39–40 years old, 2019–2020

"You don't choose your family. They are
God's gift to you, as you are to them."
—Desmond Tutu

1

Caron has a permanent smile. Even on bad days, she still cheeses. On good days, her smile expands so wide that it wraps around her face, her nostrils flare and her eyes disappear, and you can see each and every tooth in her mouth, even the third molars tucked all the way in the back.

Caron walked into my little makeshift office that doubled as a sneaker room for *retroed* versions of all of the Jordans and Air Max and Barkleys and stood in front of the TV, that's wrapped by my favorite books, the books that helped me grow into the right person for her. I could tell she was struggling to hold up that eight-pound smile. I looked up from my laptop and caught her staring at me, with tears in her eyes.

All I could think was, *Damn, why am I so good at romance? What great deed did I do now?* I'd been getting the expanded version of that smile a lot lately because I'd been doing all the things that good fiancés do: listening, taking responsibility for my fuck-ups, opening doors, setting up date nights, hanging around her friends, sending just-because roses to her office, more dinner dates on nights that aren't designated as "date night," and watching Lifetime movies without complaint even though the plot is always the same—some creepy white man wreaking havoc on a flawed and damaged lady who realizes just in time that she can defeat the creep and live happily ever after with a guy who was in the friend zone instead.

Most importantly, I'd been doing the one thing that I struggled with my entire life, even after reading bell hooks over and over again: openly sharing my personal feelings. And I did it no matter how goofy or embarrassing it felt.

"What's wrong?" I asked.

"Baby," she said. "I am—we are—we are pregnant."

I leaped up and wrapped my arms around her, pulled back to say, "For real, baby, we having a baby, baby?" and pulled her bone deep into my world again, squeezing her tiny shoulders, rocking back and forth.

In that moment, as our bodies clung together like magnets, a new kind of fear kicked in—a burning fear drenched in uncertainty that both warmed and froze my chest. I squeezed her tighter. She cried more tears while probably saying some deep, memorable things that I should've been listening to or even writing down. But I didn't really hear anything after "We are pregnant."

Not because I get weirded out when couples say "we" are pregnant—as if men have to deal with swollen feet, picking up an extra thirty to fifty pounds, craving tuna mixed with grapes and chocolate cookie dough, while having to prepare themselves mentally and physically to push out a small, slimy, breathing human that they carried around for nine months, no. The fear of being someone's father just drowned out everything that came next.

I was on the wrong side of thirty, with clicking knees and aching joints, and not to mention we weren't yet actively planning on a pregnancy. Sure, we'd talked about it; however, nothing was etched in stone. Jokingly, we had laid some pretty heavy hypothetical plans, in that way you do when it's all still hypothetical. As parents we decided we'd be loving and caring, open and fun—parents our kids would want to hang out with and even dress like, the parents their friends would want to hang out with. We'd be the parents who would make reading and math fun, spinach and lima beans cool. The parents who would make all the other parents say, "You want to stay over at the Watkins house again? Are they starting a cult over there? What are they slipping in your almond milk?"

Before we were expecting, Caron and I would joke about our parenting skills over half-eaten plates of food and empty red-wine-stained glasses. With our feet kicked up and our egos as full as our bellies, we'd go on and on, because we just knew that if we had kids, we'd be the parents they could bring any and every issue to without fear. We'd be the parents whose kids—from infancy through the teenage years—had zero effect on our romance. The parents who would never have disagreements with our kids, because our family would be so perfect.

It's funny how people without children are always experts on parenting. But now that a baby wasn't hypothetical but an impending reality, we had to try to become those impossibly perfect parents, and that was scary.

Being in control of someone else's whole life—where they live, what they eat, how they're socialized and educated, their health, their influences, their safety—without instructions was the scariest thing I had ever faced. This unborn baby's well-being owned my thoughts; as soon as I woke up in the morning, while having my eggs and coffee, while I worked, after work, during dinner, and before I fell asleep. I was preoccupied with everything unknown about the baby, everything that scared me about life.

———

"D. Watkins from east Baltimore" is how I'm often introduced, and the affiliation with my neighborhood makes me
smile. Being from east Baltimore to me means resiliency,
heart, grit, and a willingness to take chances that would bind
up most people from other places in fear.

One time in North Carolina, right outside of Durham,
I mouthed off to a pack of angry box-shaped white cops,
telling them, "Fuck you!" Daring them to touch me repeatedly, crossing the line while their right hands massaged their
pistols. "And if you shoot? You better kill me!" I continued,
as three or four people in the mix of the scene tried to defuse
the situation, while onlookers stood by with their phones in
hand, itching to record a BLM murder.

Writing has indirectly taken me all around the world,
and given me plenty of opportunities to expand on this idea
of being east Baltimore fearless. In Cairo, Egypt, I paid a
taxi driver a stack of Egyptian pounds to let me wheel his
car around so I could feel like a local. I skipped signals,
we both gave other drivers the finger, and I bumped like
thirty cars before going back to the neighborhood my hotel
was in and drinking the night away. I once walked through
Abuja, Nigeria, weeks after the United Nations building was
bombed, even though the host begged me not to explore the
town, even though most of the visiting artists were scared to
leave the Transcorp Hilton with me, even though I could still
smell the smoke as I exited. Why? I'm from east Baltimore,
and I'm not supposed to be scared of anything, even when I
am. You know, the lie.

A child meant that I'd have to confront my past. The past
harrowed me, speaking about it made me physically ache. To

have a baby meant that I had to admit to the chaos that had developed me. I was a kid who loved to fight. I'd throw anything out of a window that would fit, from dining room chairs to Easy-Bake Ovens. I found adrenaline in riding a dirt bike up and down Ashland Avenue through Miss May's back door, only to spin around in her kitchen and wheel back out down the steps. That was normal for me. I thought no one cared. I didn't feel protected at home. Hugs and hearing "I love you" were rare at home. Now I'd have to create a home, and I wanted one where "I love you"s were heard every day.

My anger, my attitude, my outbursts, my addictions, my block, my crack sales, Dad in rehab, Dad relapsing, Dad rolling out, Dad coming back; my guns, gunplay, gun work, being on the right side of pistols, death; the overdoses, the raids; more deaths again and again and again. I was lucky enough to have crawled out without losing my mind. I called those times the bad years when talking to Caron, as if they were that far behind me, but in every man's life there comes a time when he can no longer hide from the past, and the demons it carries with it, they must be made sense of.

"What are you thinking about?" Caron asked, looking up from our hug. "What's on your mind?"

Before I found out Caron was pregnant, I was also the "D. Watkins who's never leaving east Baltimore." Navy SEALs in full armor with orders from the president couldn't drag me out. The streets, or my other dad, are part of me: every section, every block, from my origin Down-Da-Hill on Robinson, to Curley Street, Deakyland, 1020 Durham, Madeira Street with Nick, the stash house with Troy, Mom's crib and Up Top; to Chapel Hill to Greenmount, to Zone 18, over to the tree-lined blocks of Ednor; the couch in Latrobe where I ate instant oatmeal four times a day, every day, while waiting for my first book advance, then off to Calvert Street, right off 20th. East Baltimore.

East Baltimore was home.

I hadn't stayed in public housing for a few years now, but I'd stayed close—maybe a $3.27 Uber ride away from the chaos and drama where I thought I pulled my resiliency from. I could still keep tabs on who got shot and locked up or who was on their way home after a ten-year stretch, but I was far enough to take sanity breaks when I need them. My neighborhood was cool, not too flashy, and low-key, full of a bunch of up-and-coming artists, waiters, writers like me, and I guess what you would call lower-working-class people. We were all too busy grinding to get into somebody's business and lived close enough to a collection of restaurants, bars, and event spaces, which was perfect for me. I was a few blocks away from Penn Station, so if I had to venture to New York to do book stuff it was easy. I had no plans to leave this part of the city, until Caron told me she, or we, were pregnant.

In fact, that day she told me, I started looking for houses with yards in one of the safer east Baltimore neighborhoods, like Charles Village with the beautiful brownstones or Original Northwood in northeast—maybe a $9.78 Uber ride from the blocks of my youth. I don't even know why I suddenly cared so much about having a yard, I never had a yard in my life—but it seems like good parents do. I decided my son— we both agreed that we were probably having a boy—would have a house with a nice yard, in the safest east Baltimore neighborhood.

I imagined myself now a retired street guy with those flimsy brown leather sandals dads wear and a corny apron that read "Kiss the Pitmaster." I'd probably point at the corny "Kiss the Pitmaster" graphic every time Caron walked by and expect a peck on the cheek for being so wonderful. She'd probably do it because she's just as square. I'd proudly throw my pitmaster apron on every weekend and smoke chicken, grill veggie hot dogs and Beyond Burgers because we don't eat pork ribs, while Caron whipped up seafood salad, the real kind with big shrimp and $40-a-pound lump crab meat, not that shit Burger ate. That's the life I'd give my son. After dinner we'd play catch, and I'd yell, "Go long, Junior!" before hurling a football thirty yards across my huge nonexistent backyard. The neighbors would watch in awe, wanting me to play catch with their son too.

I thought about our son constantly: *How can I keep him from the streets? He will be into books early and he's never going to any camp, fuck that.* Despite the ups and downs I had with my own father, I wanted my son to feel the same kind of father-son bond and love.

I'd spend all day super nervous and tense until I got to lay next to Caron, placing my hand on her bare stomach, feeling the way he balled up in her. When I would be restless and couldn't sleep some nights but she was, I felt him poking around in her belly, stretching, squirming like he was trying to force his way through to me.

"Let's not name him after me," I said, on a car ride to a doctor's visit. "I want him to have his own identity." I like that I'm named after my dad; however, I do feel like that affiliation has not always paid dividends. I know some people loved me or did not like me, all because they knew who my father was, and I just feel like both were unfair. My son deserves the opportunity to earn his love and hate.

"I totally agree," Caron responded. "But I would like for him to have my initials. You know I have my mother's initials, right? It's a family tradition."

"What do you have in mind?" I asked.

"I like the name Cross."

"Cross." I looked at her, googling the standard definition of the word. "Cross means commitment to faith. Cross Watkins, I like it."

"I'm pretty sure we are having a boy, but what if it's a girl?" Caron said. "I also like the name Genesis, even though it would break the initial tradition."

"Boy or girl," I answered, "I like the name Cross, it feels right."

"Cross," she said.

"Cross," I echoed.

On a doctor's visit, a woman in blue scrubs, maybe some type of nurse or ultrasound tech, waved a sonogram image at us, closely looking.

"Do you guys want to know what you are having?"

"Of course we do!" we both said in our own way. We aren't big on surprises.

The woman took a closer look, squinting her eyes into slits while opening her mouth wide. "Girl. It's a girl."

Caron and I locked eyes.

"Are you sure?"

"Well, not 100 percent, but, yeah, it's a girl."

We busted out laughing. We had a great visit, the doctor said everything looked good and we had nothing to worry about. Knowing that we were having a girl made me happy in an unexplainable way, and visibly, Caron shared in the joy. Every conversation went from the baby to *Cross this* and *Cross that* and *Cross, Cross, Cross*, we were Crossed out—and the joy I felt could only be connected to the feeling I had when Caron cried "Yes" after I proposed, or when Caron told me she was pregnant, or the first time I laid eyes on her on Coppin's campus long ago. Cross was us.

2

A girl.

I am having a daughter. When I thought of our future child as a boy—a little version of me—I imagined him being just like me, handsome, smart, and able to handle anything. Most of the men I hung around fantasized about having a male child, somebody to carry the name. I didn't have a preference, but a girl seemed easier to raise than a boy. As much as I thought that I'd now evolved beyond stereotypical ideas of masculinity, I couldn't help but think that as a boy my whole life and the foundation of my success was built on a toughness, a deep-seated grit, so deep that it's still a part of me no matter how much I try to soften to this new life, of being a husband, and now a father. How could I have a son that needed hugs, affection, and the kind of nurturing that I had yet to figure out? Having a daughter seemed easier, almost an exciting relief. But I would still be raising her in Baltimore, which would present its own challenges.

And I knew that one day somebody was going to recognize her last name and say something like, "Your father, D. Watkins, is an amazing person. He donated copies of his books to my school, and we read them front to back twice over. He visited us multiple times, funded pizza parties, and passed out thousands of dollars in gift cards. He is the first real author we ever met. He taught us the power of critical thinking and is the reason why I decided to become a writer. He not only told me and showed me that I can do it, but he also helped me start my career. I love D. Watkins. He's the best."

I also knew that one day somebody was going to recognize her last name and say something like, "Your father sold drugs with Troy and the girl Tweety in front of my grandmother's house. He hung with guys like Nick and Burger who banged guns in the neighborhood all night long. He paid fiends to put on boxing gloves and beat on each other for his own selfish entertainment. And when he wasn't paying the fiends, those same fiends robbed and stole from us because they had to get high off of his drugs. He helped bring all of that violence into our neighborhood and we had to survive that. Fuck D. Watkins. He's the worst."

Both of those people would be absolutely right.

My backstory is one of both pain and healing. I would have to explain to Cross that nobody is just one thing. People are complex, walking contradictions.

Lying on Caron's belly, I thought about whether we should raise Cross in east Baltimore. It felt like an oxymoron. Baltimore is also a contradiction.

My work, my life, is still in east and west Baltimore. She'd have to know east Baltimore to know me, and I'd want her to know the real me. I shop at the same stores and hit up some of the same watering holes; chill with the change-makers of east Baltimore as well as the ones who are in need of change. She will witness this duality of my life and work throughout hers. I shifted my body to listen closer for Cross's heartbeart, thinking about my daughter playing a part in my work in Baltimore, being a part of the change, carrying on my legacy.

Maybe I would take Cross with me to visit the schools that I'd given books to, or even attend them, maybe Cross would want to spend time in my old neighborhood and carve out her own identity there, be part of the duality of my world, of the world most Black people live in, navigating the different spaces of our existence and the complications and beauty of them all.

I wanted to ask Caron if we should move back to east Baltimore for Cross, but then I thought about things like the school district. But fuck a school district, shouldn't I be encouraging her to see the humanity in the place that I continue to fight for the world to see? Wouldn't the truest test of my impact and loyalty to east Baltimore be to let it be a place where I'm comfortable raising my family, with my own kids playing freely in the same streets I ran? I didn't want to be a phony, become some dude who warned his daughter to keep her away from guys like me—we were the ones who switched the negative to positive. We were the ones doing stuff for the community that no one could see, truly loyal to the betterment of our people on a daily basis, whether giving out gift cards or books, we chose to remain in the fire of east Baltimore. Could Cross truly understand that fire from afar?

I wanted to think she could, no matter where I raised her. But I'd also have to understand if she didn't. Her background was going to be different from mine. She won't be from the same block that raised me, she won't have the same level of emotional investment. What she would have instead is stability—along with amazing schools, a fridge full of fresh vegetables, parents who talk about art, yearly trips, a savings account, and activities from karate class to magic class, or dance class, or whatever kind of class she wants. I had amazing parents, considering how young they were when they had me, and I loved my block, but she would have all of what I didn't have. The kind of safety I never dreamed of as a kid. If giving her the gift of that safety meant leaving my beloved home, living outside of my zone of familiarity, away from the origin of my resilience, I decided right there on Caron's lap that I was okay with it. I was still D. Watkins from east Baltimore. In time she would have her own Baltimore contradictions to reconcile, for better and for worse.

———

Being a Black man in America is exhausting. I've always been a Black man in America, so I don't have anything to compare it to. I'm likely to be shot by a cop; one out of four people who look like me are convicted of a felony at some point and must work extra hard for opportunities that white men easily consider standard or normal. All of this struggle is my normal; it was only through a combination of luck and aggressive planning that I was able to carve out a bit of success. Yet the privilege of my gender grants me more of America. I'm still a member of the boys' club in many ways. If we were having a boy, I would already have had a blueprint for teaching him how to survive this system as a Black man, understanding the stereotypes, respecting women, and aggressively fighting for what you deserve regardless of who disagrees. But now I'd have to teach Cross how to navigate a society that specializes in both racism and sexism.

It troubles me that Cross will be starting her life in a country where Black women are paid 61 cents for every dollar paid to white men; where no matter how talented, resilient, and strong Black women are—like she will be, and the women in our family are—they are still underrepresented in leadership positions across the country. Black women also represent almost half of the low-wage workforce, and are two times more likely to go to prison than white women who commit the same crimes. Cross will be coming into a world where Black women are three to four times more likely to die from pregnancy-related causes than white women. Study after study shows that life for Black girls in America is not fair.

I buried my head in Caron. "You okay?" she asked.

"Yeah," I said. But I was afraid for Cross. She'll be confronted with the stuff that doesn't necessarily make it into the studies, like the widespread demonization of Black women's hair, which starts as early as elementary school with discriminatory dress codes and continues up into the workplace, smearing many Black women's hairstyles—from extensions to braids, from locs to afros—first as "distracting" and later as "unprofessional." I don't want her to experience a world where her hair isn't good enough, and needs to look more like a white girl's hair, because white girls have "normal" hair. A place where normal white girl hair is everywhere, too: all over television, in magazines, and even in children's books, which too often lack Black heroines. Raising Cross is going to require the explanation of a lot of things that we should not have to explain. I once Googled "beauty" and got pages and pages of images of blonde white women.

I'll have to explain why to Cross one day.

"I'll have to explain to Cross how algorithms are racist and sexist," I said suddenly to Caron. "How can one group of people own beauty?"

But I'm lucky that I don't have to do it alone. Caron is more intelligent than me—except when we play Scrabble. She will undoubtedly be our daughter's biggest superhero. I closed my eyes and saw the relationship they would have: girl talk, debates, and ice cream dates; playing dress-up and making fun of me when I burn their pancakes. Cursing me when I attempt to braid Cross's hair and then loving me for trying. Knowing our daughter's life will be blanketed by Caron's guidance and love helps ease my fears of raising a Black daughter in this country, as does the faith I have in the love I have to offer.

But my first objective as a dad was to find every book with a Black princess as the protagonist and adding it to our Cross library, I thought to myself. There's a library in our living room and the one I'm making in the basement.

"I'm going to spoil her ridiculously." I looked up at Caron this time and she shook her head.

"I'm not going to let you spoil her too much," she laughed, holding her belly. "She's going to have you wrapped around her finger."

"I'm an old dad, pushing forty. I'd love to spend my remaining years making you and her smile. That makes me smile. Let's move the wedding up."

"You sure?" Caron looked intrigued, not concerned or excited. She was wondering if I was serious.

"Yeah." I wanted to make it official. I was excited about our family. I loved Caron and I didn't feel a need to wait, and I could see in her eyes that she didn't either. I'm not old-fashioned, but I wanted to do family in a way my parents didn't.

"Great, we don't have to pay for a big wedding where I have to be all big and pregnant and sober while everyone else is on the dance floor drinking and having a good time!" Caron was in.

"Hell no!" I laughed.

———————

The Watkinses, I think to myself. It's August 8, 2019, and we're in Canton, at the same waterfront where I proposed, in southeast Baltimore at 6 a.m.—a metaphor for the sun rising on our new life. We are surrounded by close friends and family. Caron is the most beautiful bride I have ever seen. Her dad slowly walks her down the aisle toward me. She's wearing that big beautiful smile, identical to the first time I laid eyes on her at Coppin. When it approaches me, I realize it's the smile that I always wanted beside me, and I want to hold on to it for the rest of my life. The pastor, her uncle, officiates. He asks the questions, and we both proudly say, "I do."

It's simple, just like us.

The Watkinses.

3

8 p.m.

It's January 14, 2020, I'm sitting at a table at Motor House, the studio/bar where one of my best friends, photographer Devin Allen, hosts a monthly Artist Talks series. I keep an eye on my phone waiting for a text from Caron as I wait for my turn on stage, while friends and friends of friends bring rounds of drinks around. The mood is celebratory but we aren't celebrating anything specific, exactly. It's not a particularly special day in America, but every day above ground in Baltimore is kind of special. We're a relatively small city with an extremely high murder rate, and we had just closed out 2019 with 348 homicides.

At this event, Devin interviews local creators onstage over drinks. A group of artists, including me, had been invited that night to recap the work we did in 2019 and share what we were planning for 2020. Liquor is flowing in streams and running in every direction at this event, so I couldn't have asked Caron to endure that. The plan is for me to hit the venue, give my portion of the talk, and, by the time I am set to leave, probably get a text from her telling me, *Hey baby, bring a shrimp sub home.* It was getting close to her due date, and I wanted to be home with her.

"Baby, text me if you want something else to eat, a shrimp

sub or something," I had said to her on the phone before heading to the venue. "The event shouldn't be that long. I'll be right home afterwards."

"Don't drink too much," she warned.

I probably should've stayed home, though. We don't know that she is already in labor.

"Yoooo, bro!" I hear. "Didn't know you was coming out tonight!"

My good friend Dee Dave, a popular Baltimore rapper who's always grinning and hungry to trade ideas, goals, and plans, walks up on me wearing a cool letter jacket that I jokingly tell him I'm going to steal.

"Surprised you ain't out on tour knocking those books off," he says. "I gotta read ya new one. I'm honored that you put me in there!"

"Come on man, we family," I reply. "And I'm home for now, bro. My baby girl will be here any day now."

His big eyes grow bigger and he gives me a pound, then a firm hug.

"That's love, bro! No better joy than being a father! Come on, lemme grab you one!"

Elbow- and excuse-me-room-only wait in the section where the bar is located, each and every wall lined with paintings floating over seasoned and up-and-coming artists alike. If you wanted to delete the art scene in Baltimore and the bulk of its fans, all you have to do is drop a bomb on Motor House that night. Lucky for me and Dee Dave, we don't need to worry about drinks; Devin's event sponsor has supplied more than enough for his featured artists.

"Devin!" I call out, pulling him away from three conversations. "Put me onstage ASAP, bro. I gotta get home!"

---

9 p.m.

I'm pinned against the wall now, with six rounds of drinks lined up in front of me—some clear, some brown, some mixed—and a bunch of yelling, rapping, laughing, celebrating, weirdly dressed people trying to make me play catch-up, daring me to drink this and drink that. I hold my initial cup and sip slowly. As they talk and joke and prep to sit down with Devin onstage, I slowly give away the drinks they've lined up for me to other people, or even back to them as if I bought that round, and they don't even notice.

"Yo, we headed up to the stage," Dee Dave tells me. "Let's go!"

I sit back and watch Dee Dave with one of his rap partners—and my close friend—FMG Dez join Devin on stage. They talk about rap, life, family, and the love they have for our city. Dee Dave shares his victories and welcomes his struggles in the music industry with insurmountable love. "So many people quit," he says, "so many artists stop; I can't imagine that!" His words hit home with me, they shed light on how my soul feels as a writer. He leaves me with a new hunger to be better, and I'm filled with a sense of urgency. Energized, I hit the stage a few minutes later with that same fire, following his lead in an effort to motivate myself and the audience. After my talk, Dee Dave and I finally grab that drink and toast to the moves we plan on making that year. I feel great! I made it through the night, hitting my two-drink max, but one more wouldn't hurt.

"Yo, remember you made my album a couple years back?" Dee Dave laughs. "We gotta bring you back!"

I laugh too. "Yooooo, lemme rap next time, man, I'm ready!"

Four years ago, I'd recorded an intro on a Dee Dave track called "Take It Away." I didn't really have a plan before I entered the studio, and I'm not much of a rapper, even though I consume the music religiously. He told me to say something off the top of my head, so I came up with this:

"We from east Baltimore, man, so something's gonna happen to you. Somebody's gonna try you, you might get fucked up, you might fuck somebody up, you might get shot—but you gonna go through something. We got a whole lot to accomplish in a little bit of time. So what am I doing out there, if it's not benefiting me, my family, or my team…"

"Yo, I gotta lil freestyle showcase coming up next week," Dee Dave says. "You should come, bro!"

"I'll be there," I say as I toss up a peace sign and head to my car.

I get a text from Caron: hey baby, bring a shrimp sub home

———

10 p.m.

I order a fried shrimp sub with everything on it and extra hot peppers, or what we call "Hots," from Bella Roma over in the Hampden section of Baltimore. I get home to Caron and present it to her like it's an Academy Award. She looks really pleased, and then not so pleased. Her stomach's upset, she says; her appetite came and left, and maybe tried to come back again.

———

10:30 p.m.

She sits down and starts peeling the paper and foil off of the sandwich. "I'm really not feeling well," she says through munches. "Something's different. These contractions are picking up. You think we should go to the hospital?"

"Hell yeah, let's go!"

We had prepared for this moment: nine months of reading, talking, praying, thinking, planning, overplanning, making a playlist for the baby, naming the playlist after the baby. We made a packing list for an overnight suitcase for the hospital: night clothes, special breastfeeding bras, a Bluetooth speaker, scented candles, a lighter, a diffuser, and books. But we hadn't gotten around to actually packing any of it. We throw it all into a suitcase, toss it into the back of my truck, and go. Caron tries to eat the sub as we make our way to the hospital. She knows this might be her last chance to eat for a while.

———

11 p.m.

I drop off Caron at the main entrance to the labor and delivery area of the hospital and park in the garage, conveniently located two thousand miles away. I drag the suitcase through the maze of the hospital and join my wife in a small examining room.

My heart is pounding, my stomach is flipping back and forth, back and forth. Is this it? Are we really doing this? Am I about to be a father?

They tell us she has only dilated two centimeters, which isn't enough to really do anything. We can't stay, but the nurse tells us not to check out, either. "Walk around the hospital and see what happens," she says with a wink. The wink means we should go home and chill because the baby isn't coming. But just in case she is, and we have to come back, we'd already be checked in.

1:30 a.m.

We try to relax. Maybe we try to watch a movie or maybe we watch Ice-T and Lieutenant Benson take down a rapist for the two millionth time on *Law & Order: SVU,* or maybe they watch us because Caron's tossing and turning, walking back and forth, in and out of the bathroom, up and down the steps, and apparently the hospital staff moved too fast when they sent us home because the baby is definitely coming now.

"She has to be," Caron says. "It's time."

We were expecting her in late January—the twenty-third, to be exact. Apparently she was going to follow her own agenda.

---

4 a.m.

Back at the hospital, we learn Caron is four centimeters dilated. The baby is taking her sweet little time, but she's coming.

A snarky little blockhead nurse comes into the room and starts explaining the epidural procedure. My wife had planned to try to deliver our daughter unmedicated but wants a minute to weigh her options, and nurse blockhead basically tells her to get the epidural or go home.

Caron isn't against epidurals. Birth plans change all the time. She just wants to make sure she's making the right decision for her body. The nurse rolls her eyes and starts explaining the birth of a child to us as if we are children. I'm a writer, Caron's a lawyer, and we're both certified shit-talkers, so that ends quickly and poorly for the nurse.

Caron chooses the challenge of an unmedicated birth.

"Do you know what that means?" the nurse asks again. "Do you understand what you are saying? Have you taken a birthing class?"

"Yes, we took one here, at this hospital," Caron says.

We stand on the decision and dismiss nurse blockhead. And we refuse to let her kill our vibe.

---

7 a.m.

This time, a really sweet team of nurses rolls in like three angels, smiling and nodding in unison. Their energy is calming—just what we needed after defeating the epidural lady in the previous room. They tell us everything is going to be okay and champion Caron for opting for the unmedicated birth before exiting in a row, saying they'll be back shortly.

We decide to pray.

---

10 a.m.

The three nurses come back into the room to break Caron's water.

I always thought the breaking of the water would be this big production—a stream of fluid bursting out like a geyser, or a broken fire hydrant washing us all across the room. I probably watch too much TV. When it happens to Caron, I don't really see anything.

I set up the music and crack on the diffuser. A lavender scent fills the air, calming us even more as we wait. I light candles to heighten the effect, but one of the nurses says that's a no-no. "You're going to set the smoke alarms off."

———

11 a.m.

Caron breathes.

———

12:30 p.m.

I walk up the hall to get an Einstein Bagel sandwich because I'm starving and the nurses say we are going to be a minute. When I get back, bagel and egg grease smeared all over my mouth, like a pedestrian, I watch her glow, breathe, and run toward the pain in a mystical, unimaginable way.

———

1:15 p.m.

I witness magic. Pure magic.

Caron vibes to the music, bopping her head and singing along to the R&B playlist. She smiles through tears. She breathes. She talks to the baby while rubbing her stomach, telling her that everything is going to be okay. She asks if I'm okay, as if I deserve that. It isn't about me, it's about her and our child, but she still stops to consider me even as I can't even begin to understand what her body is going through, the fight she's in to bring our baby into the world.

"Are you okay? You are doing so well!" I say, though I grow more terrified by the minute. I don't want my wife to die, or our baby to die, and this happens to Black women far too often in this country, so often that I had to stop reading articles about the dangers Black women face during childbirth.

The nurses come in and out to check on her, and we love them more by the minute. "I hope this baby comes before they get off work!" Caron says.

"Nah, for real, though," I reply, "we don't need any bad energy around us."

Caron relaxes. Overwhelmed with everything, I've tired myself out, and I fall asleep. Her mom arrives and I wake to watch Caron squatting over a yoga ball, still breathing, still vibing, still magical. She moves between the bed and the yoga ball and back to the bed as the contractions grow stronger. I make jokes—not corny dad jokes, good ones to lighten the mood.

Family comes in and out, but Caron makes it clear that she only wants me, those sweet storybook nurses, and the doctor in the room when it's time to push the baby out. That gives me the task of kicking everybody else out of the room while maintaining peace.

————

5:35 p.m.

The labor is starting to get the best of Caron. She's physically exhausted, having been in pain for more than twenty hours, and after walking around, trying various positions, and eating fifty popsicles, they keep saying she still isn't dilated enough. At this point, getting an epidural seems like the best option. Then the nurses check one last time and she's ten centimeters.

"Go get my mother," Caron says, and I run to the lobby, grab her mom, and we come right back to the delivery room.

————

5:50 p.m.

I don't know how science works, but we had been told that the doctor won't be coming in until almost six, and maybe the baby is listening because that's when she peeks her little head out.

Small dark curls peer into the world. My heart pounds. Everyone in the room scatters into their positions. Mine is to Caron's left, and her mother on the right.

"Are you going to cut the cord?" the doctor asks me.

"Of course!"

The world stops and all I can do is tell Caron how amazing she is, how proud I am as she pushes, pushes, pushes, pushes, and then gives one more glorious push, bringing our baby into the world.

The baby is so tiny it's scary—pale as soy milk, with noodles for arms, noodles for legs—and she's speckled with fluid and not breathing.

I check Caron to make sure she's still breathing, and she is. The doctor calls our baby beautiful, hands me the scissors, and tells me where to cut. *Is she alive?* I snip and they take the baby to the other side of the room to examine her. I follow.

She looks even smaller here, and she's still pale. But this time her eyes open, and then she winks at me and lets out a small scream. For the first time in a really long time, I cry. I cry for her, I cry for Caron, I cry for our family, our pain, our journey, the times we thought we wouldn't make it, the fear of this very moment, and for the moment itself.

And Caron cries as she holds her baby for the first time. She did it—twenty-two hours of love, labor, prayer, music, and good people. Cross Ashlyn Watkins—five pounds and one ounce, 18.5 inches—comes into the world on January 15, 2020, at 5:50 p.m.

With tears falling, I walk over to hold Caron, holding Cross, and we cry together. Never have I felt freer—free from anxiety, free from fear, free to cry, free to be my truest self. Free. Caron and Cross have delivered the ultimate gift of freedom. My family has freed me.

epilogue

"You know what, lil baby?" I say to one-year-old Cross. "Men who aren't married don't vote and are more likely to get gum disease because they don't have wives who make them vote and go to the dentist. Before your mom I didn't vote or have gums in my mouth."

Cross, who looks just like a mini Caron, answers with her mother's smile, "Eat! Eat!" or "Stinky!" showing all six of her little white teeth. Or she just cackles at my theories of randomness, stomping both of her feet to the tune of that hysterical laugh she inherited from both of us. I'm feeding her bananas mixed with avocado—or what we call avoca-da-boo-yaoooo—or I'm changing her. Either way, the conversation continues. "Trump's election killed the post office. I swear, we mailed the neighbor a Christmas card and she didn't receive it until Valentine's Day! And the mail lady has a small head. Cross, never trust people with small heads. Promise me you will stay away from them."

"Stinky!" Cross laughs.

When Caron leaves the baby and me to our own little world, I take the opportunity to disobey the meticulous feeding, bathing, TV, and reading schedule she's created, for no reason other than showing Cross that I'm the cool parent.

"Daddy, can I brush my teeth with ice cream?" YES!

"Daddy, can I burn your Nikes?" YES!

"Daddy, can I have two ponies?" YES! YES! AND YES!

The answer is always an enthusiastic yes.

"You know, you should never trust a person named after a city or state. I once knew a guy named Montana who bought a round of drinks for like ten people, then went to the bathroom and never came back," I tell Cross, digging through her food options. "So your mom wants you to eat this whipped-up spinach potato situation, but we can save that for when you guys hang out."

Then I pull out some grapes and blueberries, build a neat pile in front of her, and together we devour them—jamming smashed piles into our talking holes.

"When I first found out that your mom had a squealer in her belly, the squealer is you," I tell Cross, "I was super nervous, but you're so great, you make this parenting stuff easy."

"Eat! Eatttttt!" Cross replies.

When we finish with berries and grapes, we split a huge plate-sized chocolate chunk cookie. A quarter of that cookie probably holds enough sugar to shoot her small body through the roof, so I give her half of it because I want my baby to aim for the moon.

"Breakfast is as important as oxygen," I say, breaking off pieces of the cookie for her. "Lunch is really a stupid meal. When you get older, you can skip lunch for the rest of your life. I haven't had lunch since '88, and I don't miss it at all."

Cross signals for more cookies, and of course, I serve her more, a whole one if she wants it.

Once we're both loaded with enough sugar to start a refinery, I blast the Sonos to the highest level. I don't play Mom's curated church jams, instead we dance off-beat to the clean versions of Tupac, H.E.R., Jay-Z, Rihanna, NBA YoungBoy, Prince, Chaka Khan, Rick James, Drake, Teyana Taylor, Aretha Franklin, Nas, and Mary J's "My Life." When we wear ourselves out, I let her watch too much *Sesame Street*—so much *Sesame Street*. Hours of *Sesame Street*. Back-to-back episodes of Big Bird, Abby, Cookie Monster, and Mr. Noodle.

"Never, ever be like Oscar the Grouch," I tell her. "He's a hater, always mad. He lives with trash and he stinks!"

"Stinky!" she cries.

"Yes, baby!" I yell back. "Oscar is stinky!"

"Stinky!"

Cross loves that I let her binge *Sesame Street*—she even runs over and gives me big hugs in between segments before running back to the iPad to prepare for Elmo's happy, happy dance, dance. And it is in these moments, full of the smallest but sweetest affection, that I realize how much I really love her.

"Hey, Cross. I love you," I tell her after one of those big hugs. "But I don't want you to think that I just love kids. I don't like anyone else's kids. You will never see me hugging another kid. I just love you."

She runs over and gives me another big hug. I turn into a six-foot pile of lovey-dovey cupcake mush.

After bingeing a month's worth of *Sesame Street*, we spend some time throwing things from one side of the room to the other. I don't know what she can learn from this exercise, but I feel like every baby needs to learn how to throw. Tossing Legos, Snoopy, and the American Girl doll around is also a great way to burn some time while I figure out where in the world we're going to go now, because we can't just sit in the house.

I like to put her in whatever type of Jordans, Nike Air Max, or Barkleys I'm wearing that day, that is our thing. The same shoes I've chased, captured, and worn my whole life have all been resurrected into cute little baby versions for her.

We jump in the truck and cruise up and down the small blocks that make up my city, her city. Then I roll near the block where I grew up. And as we drive we slowly pass the neighborhood where me and Troy would pedal bikes through the streets all summer, where Burger beat on us, where Nick spent his last moments. Cross's presence in this place scares me, but I tell her, "This is where your daddy is from, and I'll tell you all about this place when you get older."

She looks out of her window, as if she knows what I am talking about, and maybe she does, maybe she feels it.

I tell her all about her history. I show off the old homes and tell her how all of this will be different when she's old enough to drive.

"Are you going to drive me around when you grow up?" I ask in the rearview mirror, but my antics have put her to sleep. There's the nap Caron scheduled.

When we get home, I quickly try to wash our day off of her, give her some vegetables, and get her ready for bed so that her mother can relax once she's home. We'll still wait for her for the final tuck-in, though. While we wait, I read Cross a book—*Mary Had a Little Glam* or *Hair Love*—and tell her, "I am so happy to be your father. And I will cherish these days and the days to come for the rest of my life, always pulling up for you for any and everything. And I don't care if that means I have to sit my big self at a tiny table to join your tea party, or let you paint my nails during spa day, even though I hate nail polish and how it smells, or buy you a puppy and help you raise it. I will proudly adjust to the change of you picking out my clothes and sneakers instead of me picking out yours, and that dreaded drive we will take to the movies on your first date. I'll proudly celebrate all of your wins, while being there to coach you through all of your losses. Whatever it is, I'm there."

I wouldn't want to be anywhere else in the world. We smile.

And by the end of my monologue, Caron has pulled into the driveway and rushed back into the house just to finish putting Cross to bed. But it's too late, though, because the schedule she created works too well. Even when I don't follow it, our little girl is already knocked out asleep.

But I notice I'm not the only one who breaks the rules. Caron makes a little too much noise purposely, or invents some reason to go into Cross's room, just to wake the baby up for that last goodnight kiss, too. I join them.

I love my life, because all we do is smile.

acknowledgments

First and foremost, peace God. Thank you, God, as through God all things are possible.

I would like to thank my wife, Caron, and my baby, Cross—my hearts, my biggest inspirations, I truly do all of this for the two of you.

And to my parents, Jeanie and Big Dwight, and Mo and Trey for all of the love you poured into me over the years.

Rest in Power, Devin, you remain in my prayers.

I would also like to thank my SUPER editor and publisher, Krishan Trotman, for believing in me and making this book happen, along with Amina Iro, Mikea Hughley, and the whole team at Legacy Lit.

Thank you to my manager, Brandi, and agents Barbra and Erwin for continuing to fight for me. And to my family: Kevin, Aunt Robin, Buck, Aunt Trudy, the Braces, Team Melo, Koni, Devin "Moody" Allen, Dez, Mama Koko, Alan Nelson, Andre Miles, and Darnell Baylor—thank you all for the constant energy, love, and support.

Thank you to my brother Tay Rose. Welcome home, champ, we here.

Special thanks to Nikki Giovanni, Wayetu Moore, Jason Reynolds, Mitch Jackson, Kiese Laymon, Sister Souljah, bell hooks, and Deesha Philyaw.

And to east Baltimore. To the whole Baltimore, but definitely east Baltimore.